HISTORY
OF THE
FUTURE

A C·H·R·O·N·O·L·O·G·Y

Dedicated to all
at
The Master's Press

HISTORY
OF THE
FUTURE

A · C·H·R·O·N·O·L·O·G·Y

Peter Lorie · Sidd Murray-Clark

DOUBLEDAY

NEW YORK . LONDON . TORONTO . SYDNEY . AUCKLAND

History of the Future
A Chronology
was produced by Labyrinth Publishing S.A. Switzerland
Designed by Sidd Murray-Clark and Sandipa Gould Griffin
Copyright © Text 1989 by Peter Lorie
Copyright © Original Illustrations 1989 by Sidd Murray-Clark
Copyright © *The Principles of Universal Habit* 1989
by Rupert Sheldrake
All rights reserved
Printed in Hong Kong by C & C Joint Limited
Color Separation — Fotolito Toscana, Florence, Italy
Typesetting — Parole e Immagini S.A.S. Florence, Italy
August 1989
First Edition in the United States of America

Published by Doubleday,
a division of Bantam Doubleday Dell Publishing Group, Inc.
666 Fifth Avenue, New York, New York 10103

''Doubleday'' and the portrayal of an anchor with a dolphin are trademarks of Doubleday,
a division of Bantam Doubleday Dell Publishing Group, Inc.

Library of Congress cataloging-in-publication data
Lorie, Peter
History of the Future.
1. Twenty-first century--Forecasts.
I. Title.
CB161.H62 1989 303.4'9 88-31034
ISBN 0-385-26298-1

CONTENTS

INTRODUCTION

We HAVE A HABIT OF LOOKING at the future from inside the past. It is not that we can easily do anything else — for the human mind is conditioned in such a way that what is to come remains, in the majority of minds, an extension of what has gone. We base everything on our experience — particularly in today's scientifically oriented, "rational" scheme of life.

In its place, this is fine. The future, particularly in a book like the one that follows, must be based in some sound recognition of progress — and progress comes from where we have been not from an imaginary science fiction concept.

But, just because we must be scientific and rational about the tapestry we weave of our future, does not mean we cannot be original in the way that we form our over-view of the future....

Take the works of Professor David Bohm, for example. Professor Bohm is one of a handful of brilliant physicists who have, during this century, begun to propose concepts which go beyond our normal rational thinking processes.

"The notion of spin particularly fascinated me: the idea that when something is spinning in a certain direction, it could also spin in the other direction but that somehow the two directions together would be a spin in a third direction. I felt that somehow that described experience with the processes of the mind."

Such an idea is not rational in the scientific sense. How can something spin two different ways at once? But take a look at a bicycle wheel when it is spinning. The motion forward after a certain speed makes the wheel look as though it spins backwards and yet we know it is spinning forwards. The wheel is therefore spinning in two different directions at once. It must therefore be spinning, as Bohm says, in a third way! Such concepts have a relevance to life which cannot be denied and in the coming pages we will see much of this relevance as it develops through the next centuries.

Much popular prediction takes the form of tracing existing trends within science and technology through to a highly mechanized and scientific future. We imagine the world to be something unfolding according to our rational view of the present. And yet, as we have briefly sampled from David Bohm's somewhat less obvious view of the universe, it may be that there is something completely different facing us in the coming centuries. And it is on this basis that much of the coming pages will illustrate the coming trends.

As a very general overall theme we might just look at a comparison. If we examine the maturing trend of a normal human being as our basis for world evolutionary change we can get a good picture of how life could be.

Consider the life of a young man — John Doe — who at 12 to 14 enters his "Industrial Revolution" — discovering his power as a human machine — manipulating others to meet his needs. In his teen-age years he begins the Information Revolution — the age of discovery — learning, computers, technology — the currency of converted understanding.

By his twenties he has passed through the "mass yearning for learning" and entered the age of Aquarius — the Emotional Revolution. Perhaps we can look upon our planetary evolution in the same way as we look upon a single member of that planet.

We have thus set a format of "progress" which is based on a theme of mankind's reflection in his environment. We have supposed that the whole human race, along with its various neighbors, is going to pass from what has been a fairly long Industrial Age,

closely associated with an Age of Information. If we suppose that right now we are at the center of that Age of Information and beginning to "leak" into the Age of Emotion, what then does such an age imply? Effectively, within the Age of Information, the scientist is constantly making choices and decisions. He chooses something to be interested in and he decides to interpret it. His tools for doing this work consist of language and mathematics. Language is reliant on words and mathematics on symbols. Both these "languages" are immediately restrictive for there are many things they cannot encompass.

The result is that the scientist or reductionist, proposes to declare the substance of life through a personal choice which is inevitably only a part of what is there. He makes his choice — he looks at this and not at that. And furthermore even those things he does look at are restricted by his use of language. He can only interpret according to what he already knows. Inevitably, therefore he must miss a whole lot.

The facts are sometimes accepted and sometimes not — consciously and unconsciously.

But there is more to it than this for those facts can be absorbed in two different ways. They can be taken into an intellectual labyrinth of brain tissue — processed through the computer of the brain and interpreted in whatever way the receiver wishes. This is the standard method. Or, they can be "felt", such as the concept of spin suggested by David Bohm.

In this Age of Information we spend a lot of our time making up terms like "The Age of Information" because we like to quantify and that is why we have computers, technology, incredible communication systems, space travel, genetic engineering and of course, war. We are constantly absorbing and most of this absorption takes place through the mind.

But how about the other way?

"A floor of many-colored pebbles lies beneath clear water, with fish at first noticed only by their shadows, hanging motionless or flashing through the liquid, ever-changing net of sunlight. We can watch it for hours, taken clear out of time and our own urgent history, by a scene which has been going on just like this for perhaps two million years. At times, it catches us right below the heart with an ache of nostalgia and delight compounded, when it seems that this is, after all, the world of sane, enduring reality from which we are somehow in exile.

But the feeling does not last because we *know* better. We know that the fish swim in constant fear of their lives, that they hang motionless so as not to be seen, and dart into motion because they are just nerves, startled into a jump by the tiniest ghost of an alarm.

We know that the "love of nature" is a sentimental fascination with surfaces — that the gulls do not float in the sky for delight but in watchful hunger for fish, that the golden bees do not dream in the lilies but call as routinely for honey as collection agents for rent, and that the squirrels romping, as it seems, freely and joyously through the branches, are just frustrated little balls of appetite and fear."

This quote from Alan Watts' book *Nature, Man and Woman* is full of information, but the facts that he relates can be absorbed by us in another way. We can "feel" what it is that he is saying. And what he is saying is starting to make some sense to us at the beginning of the Age of Emotion.

We *think* we know what is going on around us. But we see nature only in our own image and that is a tremendous restriction — for it gives us only part of the whole picture.

Perhaps the nervous movements of animals are not fear at all. In fact it is likely that animals do not function emotionally or physiologically like humans — not even remotely like humans.

Science and the Age of Information, in any event, have taken somewhat of a tumble recently upon the discovery that sub-atomic particles like "quarks" do not necessarily exist and yet they do not *not* necessarily exist either. They are not a certainty but only a probability! Strange to imagine that everything we are is totally founded upon something which may not be!

The very simple reason why it cannot be depended upon that these tiniest of items are in our existence, is the fact that they are so tiny that the very act of observing them changes that which is observed. And perhaps, it may be suggested, each different light particle/observer changes the sub-atomic particle in a different way.

In short, what we have today in the exactitudes of science is the inexactitude of metaphysics. Every scientist is a human being, a

8

different human being from all others of his species and so he, as opposed to the others, will see something different from the others. Thus the end of laboratory "controlled" experiments — how can you control something if the pieces of the puzzle change each time a different person is in the laboratory?!

This is something new and is the very substance of the Age of Emotions because it has to do with feelings and not reasons — the heart and not the mind.

"Everybody has seen an image of enfoldment. You fold up a sheet of paper, turn it into a small packet, make cuts in it, and then unfold it into a pattern. The parts that were close in the cuts unfold to be far away. This is like what happens in a hologram. Enfoldment is really very common in our experience. All the light in this room comes in so that the entire room is in effect folded into each part. If your eye looks, the light will be then unfolded by your eye and brain. As you look through a telescope or a camera, the whole universe of space and time is enfolded into each part, and that is unfolded by the eye." David Bohm.

Within the coming pages then, we are going to witness turns of events which will literally blow our minds, for the view of the future expressed in HISTORY OF THE FUTURE is concerned with a total break down of rational, reductionist and divisive thinking.

We will sample Rupert Sheldrake's *Principles of Universal Habit* in which he personally describes the way in which he sees his fascinating *Morphogenetic Field Theory* unfolding into the coming millennium. His proposal that these *form-fields* surround us invisibly and influence everything we do, may be extended into, for example, our understanding of memory. Perhaps there is no internal brain memory at all. Perhaps the brain simply acts as a receiving mechanism for information which exists in a cosmic state for all to draw upon.

The implications of such a theory are far-reaching to the extent that they propose that there is no past or future, only a continuous and ever-changing present. This theory has been around, in fact, for thousands of years from the Eastern philosophers such as Buddha, Mahavira and the living Masters of today such as Rajneesh and J.Krishnamurti. But we are now about to see what were originally thought of as groundless suppositions, manifesting as scientific certainties.

We shall see also the predictions of one of the world's most brilliant global financial experts — Dr. Andreas Landert from Switzerland who has provided some eye-opening facts concerned with likely trends in America and the rest of the world. Dr. Landert provides the predictions and trend graphs for *The Wall Street Journal* and many other major organizations in the world, and his view of money operates on a truly global scale. What will be the next major money-making trends? How will we use our financial power in the next millennium?

In the coming pages, as we pass through the Age of Emotions to the Age of the Heart and then into Ages of Confidence and Disaster, we will sample many strange phenomena such as *Memory Design* and *Machines that Feel*. We will see the first *World Government* and *Silence and the End of Language*, together with *Tunneling the Planet* and *The New Priesthood*. Life will pass through extraordinary trends brought about by revolutionary concepts, such as the discovery that scientists actually create their own science! It is not that science is progressive and reaches an eventual goal where it knows everything. It is that science makes problems in order to solve them — that each time a paradigm shift takes place it is because the human "observer" is actually laying its path him or herself.

And in just this way, we behave rather like gods in our game of presenting the future — for if we can imagine the future, then perhaps in this dream state, we also make it come true!

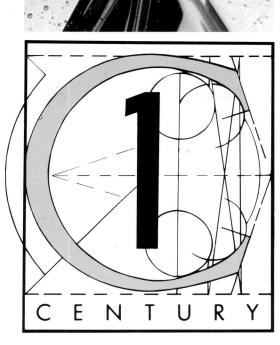

21 CENTURY

2000-2100

THE
WORLD
AS
IT
IS
— ALMOST

The trends that have begun at the end of the 20th century will flower or die at the beginning of the twenty-first. But which ones?
This is the AGE OF TRANSITION.

	THEO-SCIENCE	POLITICS-ECONOMY	MAN-SCIENCE	EARTH-NATURE	ASTRO-NOMICS
2000 · 2010	**SPIRITUAL CONNECTIONS** Science vs Non-dual thinking.			**ROOT SOLUTIONS** Breaking the patterns.	
2010 · 2020	**PRINCIPLES OF UNIVERSAL HABIT** The Fundamentals of Rupert Sheldrake.				
2020 · 2030		**WORLD GOVERNMENT EXPERIMENTS** First cooperations after 1992.	**THE GENETIC CATASTROPHE** When man meddles in unknown business.		**HAWKING-HYPE ENDS** Stephen Hawking's ideas proved wrong.
2030 · 2040	**THE NEW RELIGION** God-changes, life-changes.	**GLOBAL FINANCE** A world money-flow.			
2040 · 2050				**DEATH OF MEDICINE** Learning the true preventions.	
2050 · 2060	**COMING OF AGE** Mankind steps beyond transition.			**DOCTORS ANONYMOUS** The last traces of the MD.	
2060 · 2070	**TRANSITION'S NEW GROUPS** The new founding-fathers.	**AGRICULTURAL REALITIES** Consumption of necessities.			
2070 · 2080					
2080 · 2090			**UNKNOWN MAN** The birth of a new species.		**UNIFIED THEORY OF THE UNIVERSE** The truth is there isn't one.
2090 · 2100	**ENLIGHTENMENT SURPRISE** Master's abound.		**MAN'S DIS-EASE** The new way to sickness.		

Transition

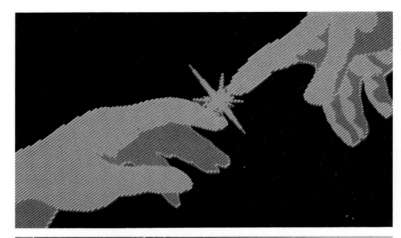

2000 • THEO-SCIENCE

Who would ever imagine
that science and religion
could come together? As
they join, man moves
forward

2010 • UNIVERSAL HABITS

Sheldrake's vision of the
20th century spreads across
vast areas of life — naming
the new Einstein

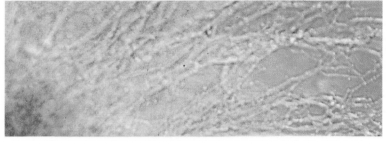

2040 • MAN'S DIS-EASE

The mechanical process of
sickness — cure from effect
ceases to be the issue.
Prevention through natural
connection clears the way

2070 • UNIFIED THEORY

The only Unified Theory of
Life is that there isn't one.
Life is a changing function
with each new discovery
producing the next

SPIRITUAL CONNECTIONS

T HE GREEKS INVENTED DUALISM, stating that everything existed with an opposite: love vs hate, good vs bad etc. This simple "mistake" has created the concept of separation for modern mankind.

And what is more significant is that we see ourselves also that way, i.e. separate from everything else. Educators and psychologists even propose that children reach a state of maturity when they separate themselves from the world they live in — in other words they begin to recognize that they are alone and against the world. It still, after thousands of years of pain and suffering, does not occur to us that no child would ever be born without Earth/nature/existence providing the place for it to happen. And that the simplest extension of this realization is that we are not separate from Earth, and not even a part of the Earth, but that we *are* Earth — one and the same and unseparated.

Science began to sample this knowledge in the last years of the 20th century, when men such as David Bohm helped expand quantum theory.

David Bohm's book *Wholeness and the Implicate Order* created a stir in the scientific community almost as big as that created by Einstein. Bohm believes that the nature of life cannot be reduced to fragments or particles but that we must take a holistic view of the universe and perceive life as a complete whole which he calls the "implicate order." Bohm's theory states that there is nothing fixed if we look upon life as a whole. Scientific experimentation therefore immediately ceases to apply. All this is still as yet theory, but by the beginning of the 21st century, it will be fact.

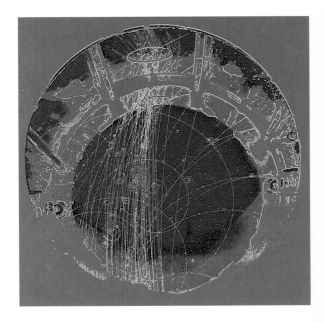

THE PRINCIPLES OF

Nature is essentially habitual. The idea grew up among the ancient Greeks that the world is governed by invisible, non-material principles transcending time and space. The Pythagoreans thought of them as numbers and numerical relationships; the Platonists thought of them as timeless ideas or Forms. These assumptions were built into the foundations of modern science, and from the seventeenth century onwards the non-material governing principles of the material universe were conceived of as immutable laws framed by a mathematical God.

Until the 1960s this old idea seemed more or less unquestionable; the universe itself was believed to be an eternal machine, and so what could be more natural than eternal laws to govern it? But with cosmological revolution caused by the Big Bang theory, the cosmos became more like a developing organism than an eternal machine. It seems to have been born some 15 million years ago, and to have been growing and developing ever since. The whole of nature has evolved; once there were no atoms, or molecules, or stars, or planets, or crystals, or living cells. All these systems have developed in the course of time. So why should we go on assuming that in an evolving universe all the laws that govern them were fixed in advance, even before the universe itself came into being?

Why not explore the possibility that the regularities of nature have actually evolved? Perhaps they depend on habits which grow up organically within the universe, rather than on laws imposed by some pre-existing mathematical mind.

The idea that the regularities of nature are more like habits than the products of eternal laws was proposed in my book *A New Science of Life: The Hypothesis of Formative Causation*

in 1981, and this thesis was further developed in *The Presence of the Past: Morphic Resonance and the Habits of Nature* (1988). This hypothesis postulates that self-organizing systems at all levels of complexity — such as atoms, molecules, crystals, cells, organisms, societies, planets and galaxies — are structured by specific fields called *morphic fields*, and these fields contain a kind of collective memory derived from previous things of their kind. Thus each aspirin crystal, for example, or each oak tree is shaped by a field which is itself shaped by a cumulative influence from the previous aspirin crystals or oak trees. This influence from previous similar systems, acting through or across both space and time, takes place by the process of *morphic resonance*, involving an action of like upon like.

This hypothesis was intensely controversial within the scientific community in the 1960s, partly because the notion of eternal laws of nature was such a deep-seated habit of thought, and partly because the idea of a new kind of action at a distance was distasteful to those who thought that all the fundamental properties of nature had already been discovered. However, there was already considerable circumstantial evidence that such a process was going on. The crystals of newly-synthesized chemicals, for example, had long been known to be hard to crystallize in the first place, but as a general rule they were seen to

UNIVERSAL HABIT

By Rupert Sheldrake

become easier to crystallize all over the world as time went on and more such crystallization was completed. It had already been found that when rats learned a new trick in one laboratory, other rats of the same breed tended to find the same thing easier to learn, even in laboratories thousands of miles away. And of course there was much evidence for the progressive improvement of human abilities all around the world, for example in athletic skills and in operating computers. Meanwhile, in psychology, the notion of a human collective unconscious was already widely accepted.

Now, in the spirit of this book, we are going to whirl ahead and see the future, at least the future as it might be.

By the 1990s, various tests of the hypothesis of formative causation will show that morphic resonance is indeed taking place. In experiments conducted under rigorously controlled conditions, new kinds of molecules and crystals will indeed be found to be influenced by the formation of the same substances in other laboratories. Chemical reactions and crystallization processes will be, as it were, *trained*, and this discovery quite soon will begin to influence the practices of the chemical industry. New processes will be run repeatedly through pilot plants before being scaled up, so that the training process can be monitored and controlled, rather than being left to chance as it was before. In the past of

this coming time, the managers of chemical engineering plants had often observed, to their surprise, that the yields of new processes increased, and indeed exceeded the calculated maximum; but until the 1990s this observation, with enormous economic implications, was treated as anecdotal, and its implications were not drawn out.

In the realm of biology, the role of morphic resonance becomes demonstrable in the development of fruit flies and other animals, in bacteria and in plants. It soon becomes clear that the genes have been greatly overrated as the carriers of hereditary information. They code for the sequence of chemical building blocks in protein and affect the chemicals that an organism can make, but they do not account for the inheritance of form and behavior, which are organized by morphic fields, inherited non-materially by morphic resonance. The discovery leads to a major revision of evolutionary theory, which for decades has been dominated by the school of neo-Darwinism, based on the assumption that heredity was explicable just in terms of genes, and that evolutionary change depended on chance genetic mutations. Unlike Darwin himself, neo-Darwinians rejected the importance of the inheritance of acquired characteristics and the hereditary effects of habits. In this sense, this new evolutionary theory, with its emphasis on the power of habit, is closer in spirit to Charles Darwin than to his 20th century followers. Indeed, the principle of universal habit enabled Darwin's insight into the role of natural selection to be extended beyond the realm of biology into all other realms of nature. Morphic fields are subject to natural selection; only successful habits are repeated again and again, and the more often they are operated, the more probable their further repetition becomes.

17

Experiments will show that animals are indeed able to learn more readily what other animals of their kind have already learned; the more that learn it in one place, the easier it becomes elsewhere. This discovery will enable a great deal of existing anecdotal evidence about dogs, cattle, dolphins and other animals to be taken seriously; people had, after all, been noticing this kind of effect for centuries, but its significance has always been dismissed by academic biologists. It will then become possible to understand the intimate interrelations between human being and domesticated animals in a new way, and to see how the training of various breeds of dogs, for example, or of horses has built up a collective memory both within the animals themselves and in the people who interacted with them. Indeed, the domestication of both animals and plants involves a co-evolution of habits both in these organisms themselves and in human beings, a process which will have a far deeper influence on the evolution of human culture and civilization than is appreciated within the era of mechanistic science.

The demonstration in the early 1990s that human learning is facilitated by morphic resonance will have had a rapid impact on the training methods used in the business and industrial sectors, as well as in the teaching of languages, musical instruments and sports. Since morphic resonance makes it easier to learn something that others have already learned, methods that maximize the influence of morphic resonance will enable new skills, both physical and mental, to be picked up much more quickly than traditional methods of teaching. The success of accelerated learning methods in the private sector will slowly influence the teaching methods used in schools, and finally even universities will begin to benefit from this new approach.

The idea that our own memories depend on morphic resonance with ourselves in the past was originally greeted with incredulity by many

scientists when it was proposed in the 1980s; the traditional assumption was that memories were stored in some unknown way as material traces within the brain. However, the repeated failure to find these hypothetical traces, together with the positive evidence for the role of morphic resonance will lead to a general recognition that our memories depend on our tuning in to ourselves in the past. We also tune in to many other people, and are influenced by the collective human memory, or collective unconscious. Insofar as we tune in to particular other people in the present, morphic resonance gives rise to telepathic communication; insofar as it is possible to tune into particular people in the past, it is possible to gain access to

inherent memory. A greater appreciation of this group memory and its power will lead to a more sophisticated understanding of political and economic realities, and will highlight the importance of national mythologies in the dynamics of peace and war. The role that morphic resonance plays through rituals — connecting past performers of the ritual with present ones, who are following the traditional procedures as closely as possible — will enable many aspects of cultural and religious life to be revalued.

The discovery which may take place early in the 21st century that morphic fields could be operated within a new kind of computer will open up a whole range of possibilities which will need considerable exploration. Two types of morphically-resonant computers will be developed — one depending on systems of liquid crystals and the other on networks of chips so thin that they are exquisitely sensitive to probabilistic quantum fluctuations. The morphic fields organize the activity of these otherwise indeterminate systems. Such machines would enable artificial intelligence to become a reality, in a way that it never could with old style computers of the 20th century. Such machines will build habits, and automatically communicate with other similar computers throughout the world, avoiding the need for telephone communications, radio links, satellites etc. They will be the precursors of an entirely new kind of technology, organic rather than mechanistic.

The principle of universal habit cannot, of course, be regarded in isolation. It is an integral part of the evolutionary, holistic world-view which has been growing up in the 20th century, but which will only perhaps come of age at the beginning of the next millennium. This new cosmology will enable us to experience the realms of science and religion as complementary rather than contradictory. Each illuminates the other in ways that are barely conceivable now.

memories of previous lives. The realization that so much of our mental life involves resonant interconnections with other people, past, present and future has implications for everyone. Not only our actions and words but also our thoughts can affect other people — even people we do not know, including those not yet born.

The appreciation that animal societies — such as colonies of termites, schools of fish, flocks of starlings and herds of deer — are organized by morphic fields will not only improve our understanding of natural history, but make us more aware of the social and cultural morphic fields within which we all live. These fields, like all morphic fields, have an

THE NEW RELIGION

SCIENCE AND RELIGION are not generally allied together. They seem always to represent opposite poles, and in fact we have adopted the scientists as the new priesthood in our desire to see all life mapped out before us. But religion is still a very important element of life and there are many people today searching for an alternative to the organized forms of religion which seem to have become little more than abstractions of the original powerful forces of the past. The hope of life is to bring two opposites together, the unreasonable and the reasonable, and then move forward.

If prophets such as Nostradamus are right, and if the old organized religions die or fall into disfavor in the next two decades, what will replace them?

Suppose that a real understanding is achieved by mankind which involves a sense of oneness with existence — that the Western approach to life and the Eastern religiousness come together. Perhaps in this New Age we would come to the conclusion that God is no longer outside our influence but firmly established within us and around us. Under these circumstances the initial response of mankind would be one of fear, that the authority of dogma was suddenly absent and there would appear to be nothing to replace it. Man would therefore be thrown back on himself.

We shall be looking more closely at this concept for the future in later chapters of this book but for the time being it is stated simply, that the way lies already established in the Human Potential Movement — a subtle and growing movement which derives its force from the personal growth of the individuals around the world who have begun to look, through meditation techniques, at individual spiritual enlightenment — at the various Masters and gurus who come, largely, from the East. But in order not to get too much into theory, we will first take a look at the practical changes we may expect in such a new world.

EXPERIMENTS
WITH WORLD GOVERNMENT

One Heart · One People · One World · One Government

PRESUMING THAT THE WESTERN CIVILIZED MAN finally becomes totally disillusioned with the political methods of the 20th century, one of the most popular alternatives to democratic, free-election administration lies in meritocracy.

Meritocracy, put simply, is government by talent. Any individual who was to be selected for what is perhaps the most important job in the world, would have to be very clever indeed — in fact would need to prove to any electors that he or she was capable of doing the job well. The simplest possible method of selecting such people is by eligibility through examination, or academic qualification. Schools and universities would be set up to qualify political leaders for the coming task and their life-time preoccupation would be through such an education, in just the same

financial organizations is currency exchange. In the year 1989 approximately five hundred million dollars was earned by only one major European bank from buying and selling currencies. This single, large diverter of financial resources would disappear completely in a world where one form of financial exchange existed. And it is this starting point which will bring us into the future predictions of the coming chapters in relation to money.

GLOBAL FINANCE

way as a scientist's career is dominated by the need to become highly qualified.

Candidates for political positions would have to be thoroughly versed in all aspects of constitutional government, financial management, social studies, psychiatry, environmental conditions and world affairs.

A shift of emphasis which proposed that the government leader was a servant of the society rather than a master would make all the difference in the world and a meritocratic system is designed for such a shift. If you pass the exams and continue to work effectively you stay in office for a fixed amount of time — one or two years. Once in office the World Government Ministers would be highly paid, and the continued eligibility for remaining in offices would be constantly monitored. In fact any meritocratic world government would operate in much the same way, with regard to the ministers and staff, as does modern industry.

We shall, of course, look more closely at the details of such a political future but briefly here we might mention the other major aspect of world government — global finance.

In the closing years of the 20th century one of the biggest money spinners for banks and

IN AN ARTICLE PUBLISHED in 1985 within one of today's most popular scientific journals a primatologist (one who studies primates) stated the following: "There's no scientific reason why you couldn't have a chimp-human hybrid." Such a statement epitomizes much of the modern genetic scientific belief and of course, within the limited sphere of science and its lack of relationship with existence, the statement is true — there *is* no scientific reason why we

THE GENETIC CATASTROPHE

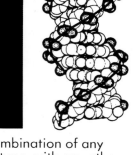

should not engineer a combination of any animal, species or living type, with any other.

The article in question goes on to state "...never completely satisfied with the gifts of nature, man has subjected the roster of species to a seemingly endless series of tinkering..and now, given recent developments in genetics and embryo transfer, the future may hold not only exciting menageries of hybrid animals but also a collection of entirely new species built one gene at a time."

The first line of this quoted piece perhaps tells the whole story — "never completely satisfied with the gifts of nature..." This is man at his present worst — regarding nature as something separate from himself, not realizing that he is therefore not satisfied with himself.

THE UN-UNIFIED
THEORY OF THE UNIVERSE

WHEN THE APPLE FELL from a tree, Isaac Newton began his inspired program for the unification of the physical universe. He created laws that predicted the forces that are now associated with gravity and the movements of the planets. He stated that light moved in a straight line and he gave much credence to many new ways of looking at physical laws.

Not so long after his laws had been accepted it became clear that his "unified theory" of life's space and matter contained a large hole.

Albert Einstein was next on the rota of genius innovators and his General Theory of Relativity proposed more sophisticated and complete visions of scientific certainty — one aspect of which was that light does not travel in a straight line but in a curved arc. And this simple change in our view of the universe has created a new picture — a new "unified theory" — which is currently once again being picked to pieces by modern science.

In his book *A Brief History of Time*, Stephen Hawking proposes that we will soon see yet another great scientific genius who will finally, once and for all find the *real* Unified Theory of the Universe. We will then be able to size up anything anywhere in any part of the physical universe — for we will have a single formula or a series of formulas that will allow us to map all existence for ever.

Such a belief is based on three things — that space, time and matter are real. That the distance between "here" and "there" really exists. That the time between "now" and "then" actually elapses and that the earth we are presently standing on and the book we are currently holding, are solid things.

ENLIGHTENMENT SURPRISE

It may be then that in the future we shall see just how real they are and how the future may begin to *real*ize that *real*ity has nothing whatever to do with theories, maps and abstractions. That in the next millennium we shall become aware of other realities which are not based on certainties, nor even prob- abilities, but on emptiness, timelessness and anti-matter. And perhaps the most likely unified theory of the universe is that there isn't one.

And finally, within the 21st century of this slowly awakening era, we will face a surprise — an enlightenment surprise — that even the five commonly understood senses do not exist as we think they do — that there is an alternative state — an altered state which we may look forward to — which we already possess but have forgotten.

CENTURY

2100·2200

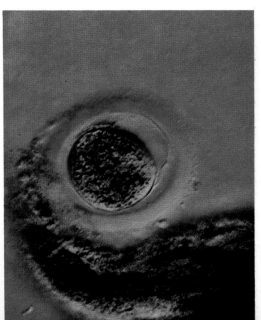

*THE
PATHWAY
TO
SURRENDER*

*In the East, life is a
pathway to surrender.
In the West, it is a
pathway to domination —
but that road has sharp
stones and must
inevitably change
direction.*

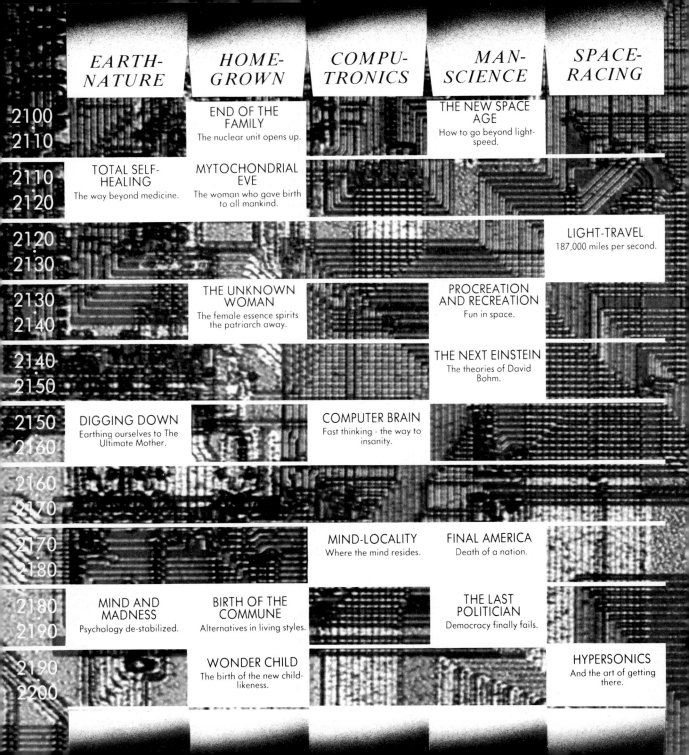

	EARTH-NATURE	HOME-GROWN	COMPU-TRONICS	MAN-SCIENCE	SPACE-RACING
2100–2110		END OF THE FAMILY — The nuclear unit opens up.		THE NEW SPACE AGE — How to go beyond light-speed.	
2110–2120	TOTAL SELF-HEALING — The way beyond medicine.	MYTOCHONDRIAL EVE — The woman who gave birth to all mankind.			
2120–2130					LIGHT-TRAVEL — 187,000 miles per second.
2130–2140		THE UNKNOWN WOMAN — The female essence spirits the patriarch away.		PROCREATION AND RECREATION — Fun in space.	
2140–2150				THE NEXT EINSTEIN — The theories of David Bohm.	
2150–2160	DIGGING DOWN — Earthing ourselves to The Ultimate Mother.		COMPUTER BRAIN — Fast thinking - the way to insanity.		
2160–2170					
2170–2180			MIND-LOCALITY — Where the mind resides.	FINAL AMERICA — Death of a nation.	
2180–2190	MIND AND MADNESS — Psychology de-stabilized.	BIRTH OF THE COMMUNE — Alternatives in living styles.		THE LAST POLITICIAN — Democracy finally fails.	
2190–2200		WONDER CHILD — The birth of the new child-likeness.			HYPERSONICS — And the art of getting there.

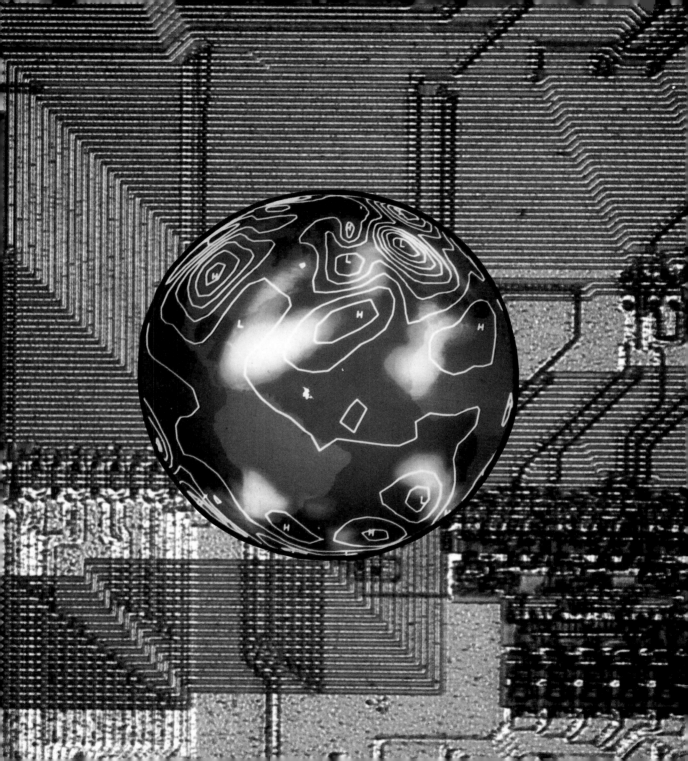

Age of Acceptance

2100 • UNKNOWN WOMAN

In the 20th century woman struggled for equality — by the 22nd century it will not be a matter of equality, she will be all and everything

2130 • MYTOCHONDRIAL EVE

Was there once one mother — a single woman who gave birth to the first man ?

2150 • MIND AND MADNESS

With the added speed of thinking created by computer brains, the mind enters states of true insanity. Cranial overload

2175 • THE LAST POLITICIAN

As world government becomes a clear alternative so democracy and its 20th century drama loses appeal

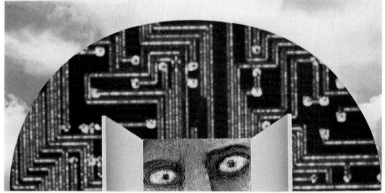

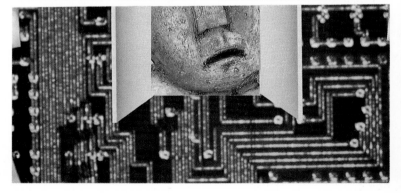

THE UNKNOWN WOMAN

WE BEGIN THIS SECOND century of the next millennium on the subject of woman. Given that the patriarchal society which has dominated the last two thousand years, is on its way out towards the end of the 20th century, we might expect something very different to replace it. It is not, perhaps that we are going to throw out a patriarchy with matriarchy, though this may be the first part of the change. It is much more that patriarch and matriarch will become meaningless in a world where manhood and womanhood are more clearly understood.

We shall be seeing this theme recurring throughout the coming centuries, but for the time being we can look at the foundations for this aspect of the future.

There is reason and some theological evidence, to suppose that there was once a "prime mother" — a woman, now known as the *Mytochondrial Eve*, who stood alone on Planet Earth millions of years ago and gave birth to the first human child. This Eve was in effect, mother to the human race and all members of that race are thought to stem from her womb.

In this respect, therefore, woman stands as the *Mother of God* — or, in other words, it was not Adam from whom a rib was taken to make woman, but Eve who gave birth to Adam.

The early millennia on Earth have needed the power and the thrust of men in order, perhaps, to push us forward, but the modern aspect of life seems now to be turning to the other side of humanity and woman-kind seems better equipped to face the next age. In this, the 22nd century, we can expect to see women in power everywhere, from government to industry, throughout the priesthood, science and technology.

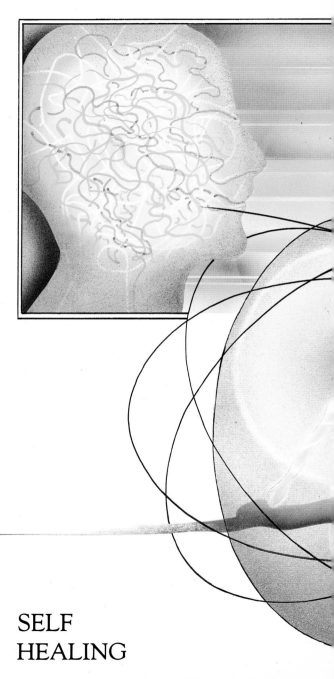

Along with changes in the political world, we will also feel the swing from "doctoring" to self healing.

The existence of incurable diseases, it will be found, arises out of two factors: the need for there to be a natural balance of population — the death rate being contained by nature through sickness and disease, and secondly the fundamental dis-ease that is related to tensions, stresses and anxiety within social conditions.

One of the fast-growing methods of helping us to understand our personal physical stresses may arise from dream states. According to a study by Stephen LaBerge of Stanford University and Jayne Gackenbach of the University of Iowa, controlling lucid dream states can put us in touch with our current physical condition. Methods and exercises have been developed to make this possible and surely by the 22nd century it is most likely that dream chambers will be available which will create the correct electronic/brain conditions for dream therapy to take place.

Another major form of self-cure will be established involving "Death Rehearsal," a technique which, during the 20th century, creates the conditions needed for a terminally ill patient to visualize what death will be like.

With a development of the current techniques being used by, for example, Alexander Levitan, a doctor at Fridley Hospital in Minnesota, the concept of understanding death will be available for healthy people also.

The fundamental understanding behind Levitan's treatments is that death is something that we can accept if we know that it is a natural biological part of life and not something terrifying and alien. Perhaps we will see, in the 22nd century, "Death Rehearsal Chambers" in every hospital.

SELF HEALING

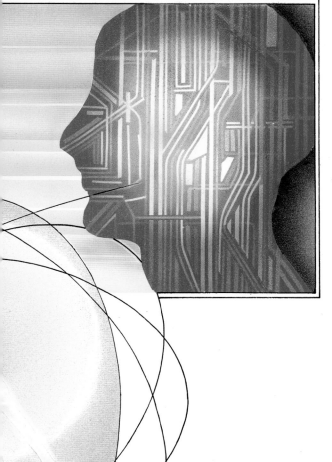

IT IS NOT UNCOMMON, during the closing years of this millennium, to hear of computer systems that will be biologically interfaced with the human brain. By the 22nd century there is little doubt that such devices will be possible and even in common use. But there is a factor in such potential which perhaps scientists may not have contemplated too seriously in their desire always to have the mind think faster and faster so that progress can advance at ever greater speeds. This concept is mind-madness.

Given the present rate of psychological sickness and the high instance of anxiety — about 34% of Americans suffer from severe mental problems of one kind or another — throughout the Western world, it may be interesting to see the increase in such problems with the arrival of the bio-chip.

The biochip was first created by a scientist named James McAlear of EMV Associates Inc., in Rockville, Maryland, U.S.A. The chip was designed as an organic molecular computer chip with a million times the computing power of its solid-state equivalent. The VSD, or Very Small Device, can be implanted in the brain and because of a coating of cultured embryonic nerve cells it links up with the nerve cells of the visual cortex, thus using the eyes as though they were a TV monitor.

The system, once melded with the human brain, sends out shoots of nerve fibers to grow

COMPUTER BRAIN, MIND AND MADNESS

into nerve cells and the "unit" contains a double helix for self-replication. Such a device is capable of storing the entire Library of Congress, and every bit of information is instantly accessible. It is believed that such a chip would even overcome death! The biochip would be removable and transferable to another body, thus bringing immortality to man's mind. Imagine how much madness such a device could bring!

REALITY
THE
NEXT
EINSTEIN

W̶E TOUCHED, BRIEFLY, during the last chapter on the likelihood of a new physics which may arise out of a fresh understanding of universal laws, or rather out of a universal lawlessness.

The centerpiece of conflict between the experimental physicists of the late 20th century and the quantum theorists seems to be the believed presence of the particle. Within the physicists, *Grand Unification Theory* there is a present need to find an illusive particle which is imaginatively named *the magnetic monopoly.* This single particle, it is expected, will tie together all the theories and experimental work and upon its discovery science will finally have all the answers — science as God.

A physicist named David Caplin of Imperial College, London University has recently come up with a possible candidate for this particularly powerful potential particle — one that he states might only appear once in every ten thousand years. Work proceeds, despite this clear disadvantage, to track and identify the final probability and make it fact.

But the other side of the coin is also making itself very visible. The theories and experiments of a small number of scientists such as Bohm, Sheldrake and others, are increasingly attractive, for they reflect the new paradigm which has only arisen in recent years.

Bohm indicates that the very basis of particle physics is on the wrong track — that the universe, seen as a series of particles, is a creation of the scientist and may not be an accurate view. As we mentioned briefly in the introduction, he indicates that if we consider the concept of spin, we can say that if something is spinning in one direction, it may also be spinning in the other direction, and that such a state would indicate a third, invisible spin. He also speaks of the universe as being *enfolded* in a certain way and that it is only our

conditioning which *unfolds* that universe in the way that we perceive it.

If we imagine that light enters a room in an *enfolded* state and our eyes/brains *unfold* that light to suit the patterns of our lives, perhaps the *unfolding* may be possible in another manner also. This same theory can be used not only to describe that which occupies space but also time. Bohm's theory extends to show that space, in its enfoldment occupies the universe in a similar fashion to the images on a holographic plate — in other words space — the whole of space — exists in all parts of it. If we look through a lens at a holographic plate we can see the whole image on the plate at all parts of the plate. He uses this as an analogy to describe that in every single point of space, the entire universe is present and only because we operate on the basis of particles do we imagine that space is like an ordinary photographic print — made up of dots. Time then can also be seen as existing in every moment — all past, present and future being here, now. The recent, past, he states, is enfolded more strongly than the distant past and so also the close future, for these items of time impinge upon our consciousness more strongly.

Such concepts are about as radical as any presented during the last years of the 20th century, but if they are developed and reach some state of mathematical persuasion then we could find them adopted into the scientific mode before the beginning of the 22nd century.

The major difference that becomes evident when studying the two persuasions is that the majority of particle-oriented scientists seem intent on finding methods of controlling the universe,whereas the theoretical "mechanics" seem much more intent on simply understanding the perceptions that are presented to them — willing to allow life to unfold in whatever way it will.

Albert Einstein, when presented with the quantum mechanical theories, was heard to say

"God doesn't play dice." It is very much part of the scientific belief that not only does science know a lot about what life is made of, but it knows how God behaves. The greater part, for example, of Stephen Hawking's book *A Brief History of Time* seems to be more a search for the meaning of God than a scientific proposal for the Grand Unified Theory. If the scientist believes, somewhere inside himself, that this search is the search for the true power of God through logic and reason, then it may be that in coming centuries he will need to accept one major factor before being able to proceed. That God *does* throw dice, and He doesn't even load them in His favor. For perhaps God knows about as much of how the universe works as does man. It is the very desire to know the answers that takes us away from them.

It is of great interest to look at the likely developments that will arise from such a fundamental change in reasoning and understanding. If the predictions are correct and we do enter a time of "unreason", of

constructive chaos through an acceptance that at the very moment science proves something to be true it changes, we will have to do some serious reappraising of our lives.

Take the very personal matter of the position of the individual within the universe. We are currently convinced that our bodies and our lives are based on some very solid foundations. We consider flesh and blood, food, furniture and facts to be things we can rely upon.

But if Bohm's concepts and the beliefs of other quantum theorists are proven accurate there may be no basis for life whatever. The mind, for example, can be seen, within these theories, as something that does not arise from individual thoughts but is a group system that occupies the cosmos and carries us humans within its arms.

If "mind" is one massive consciousness and we are simply puppets of its presence, then where do our personalities fit in? If we have no individual ego then many of our ideas about ourselves and our lives will disappear through a very unsolid window!

Perhaps during the 22nd century we will no longer be concerned so much with our own small personal problems and will begin to take a more serious interest in the whole of life — the whole planet, the whole of existence — the whole and the implicate order of things. Once the individual ego has been put in its place, life may be able to begin afresh.

OUR DESIRE TO EXPLORE and experience our universe has driven us forward so that time itself becomes simply a measure of our technological advances. We strive deeper and deeper in an attempt to understand — not to empathize, but master. And thus we view the planet as a tool and nature a device for us to exploit and use to further our own ends. However, this lust is blinding so that we explore without seeking and experience without feeling.

The ability to travel into space has the possibility of changing this process in the future. Those few people in our present time who have experienced space travel have come back with a new perception of our planet Earth. Their experience has made them realize that rather than being the planet's adversary they are in fact part of it. This realization has made these astronauts feel instead of being "an American citizen" they are "planetary citizens".

The launch of the Martian Cycler in the next millennium will be the first of the commercial links between Earth and Mars, making it possible for the first time, for mass travel between the two planets. Nick-named by its users as the Martian Metro, the Cycler will be composed of two living quarters in the shape of pyramids connected by a trusswork girder joining the pyramids at their points. The structure will spin about its mid-point to create the effect of gravity in the pyramids, the rate of rotation being controlled by weights tethered at the end of Kevlar cables at a distance of up to 15,000 feet.

The craft will travel continuously between the two planets, its 6 permanent crewpeople picking up and sending off passengers (up to maximum of 52 passengers) at the various cyclaports along the way. From these ports the passengers are able to take taxis to the many recreational areas and resorts on route.

" GOD DOES NOT PLAY DICE "

Procreation and Recreation

ALTHOUGH SPACE REMAINS virgin territory to the most intimate of human activities, sex, it can now only be a matter of time before this changes. While the majority of astronauts up to this point have been male the number of mixed crews is increasing so that it is inevitable that in the near future this frontier will finally be crossed and the membership of the "Zero G Club" will officially be opened.

The common practice of space sex will proliferate since l'amour at zero G will prove to be extremely conducive to a good sex life.

The many advantages to making love in space become immediately obvious. When weightless and in an environment where there is no up or down, the concept of going on top or underneath no longer exists and therefore neither partner ends up supporting the weight of the other. Furthermore you will no longer need to be a contortionist when you have the

desire to change position — the process will be effortless and, unlike on Earth, graceful as well! There will also be certain physiological advantages to sex in space. It is easier for the heart to pump blood through the cardiovascular system at zero G, it should therefore be easier to obtain an erection and maintain it! The same is true of course for both the male and female erectile tissue!

There will also be another important physiological difference to sex in space as opposed to on Earth — that of conception. In the absence of gravity, fertilization of the ova by the sperm becomes much less likely.

Hypersonics

FACILITATED BY ADVANCES IN engine design, materials technology, and computer aided design , the first hypersonic passenger airliner will come into service in the year 2019. This incredible craft, called Transat (short for transatmosphere vehicle) cruises just below the edge of space at speeds between Mach 15 and 25 some ten times faster than the fastest airliner in service today, Concorde. The basic version will be powered by scramjets and will fly just below the edge of space at speeds higher than

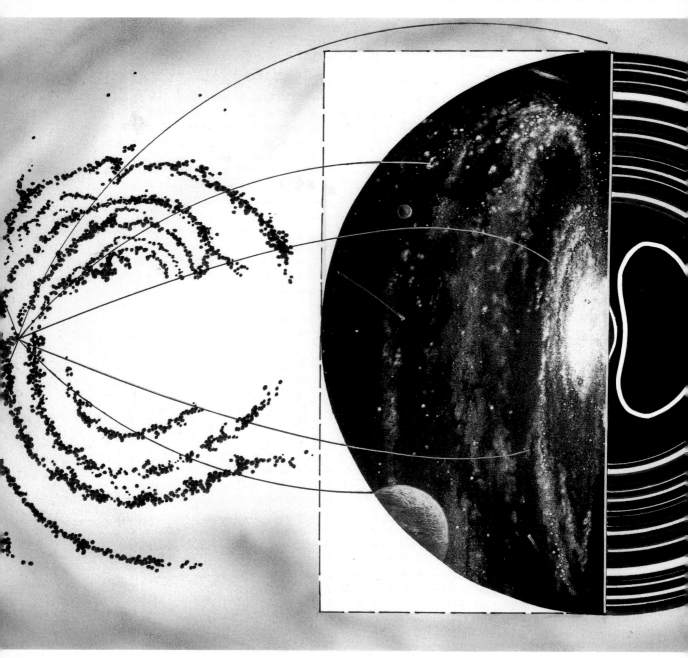

THE NEW SPACE AGE

Advertisement

Spend "no time" with us and enjoy a view that's out of this world!
Free ADVANTAGES from the nearest conveniently situated Cycloport, in one of our own fleet of luxury cyclotaxis, you can return before you even arrive!
Just 20 parsecs from earth and 100 from mars, the Scram-wonder is a passion space wagon where you can experience the many advantages of love at zero G.

Mach 15, and operate from traditional runways. A more advanced version of Transat will add rocket power to give it the extra kick needed to go into orbit from its cruising altitude. Such a craft will give a journey time of just one hour and a half between New York and Sydney, Australia!

Just as today we are beginning to see the proliferation of different rockets capable of lifting a payload and depositing it, not always successfully, into orbit, so we will see in the future many different types of planes capable of hypersonic flight. The British *HOTOL* will be powered by air-breathing rockets fueled by liquid oxygen and hydrogen. They will draw oxygen from the atmosphere during much of the climb toward either cruising altitude or orbit. This reduces the amount of propellant that must be carried on board and permits the use of the wings to optimize the initial flight trajectory after takeoff from a standard runway. Hotol will use a trolley which parts company with the aircraft at liftoff, for its takeoff role. It will have a gliding shuttle-like landing on a lightweight undercarriage. It will be a relatively small spaceplane, with a payload of just seven tons. It is called a launch vehicle though the British envisage an airline type module that could be placed into its cargo bay for piloted trips from London to Sydney taking little more than an hour.

Scramjets

IT HAD BEEN KNOWN since the middle of the twentieth century that if a ramjet could burn fuel in a supersonic airflow much higher speeds and performance could be attained.

An ordinary turbojet cannot fly faster than Mach 3, three times the speed of sound. Above Mach 3 the heat can cause engine parts to weaken. Ramjets overcome this problem but cannot take off from the ground, requiring an initial speed of 100mph. Ramjets reach peak performance at Mach 3 but efficiency drastically falls off at Mach 6 — far short of the velocity needed to orbit, Mach 24.

Scramjets will be fueled by hydrogen and will draw their oxygen from the atmosphere. Air is funneled into the the engine at exactly the correct temperature and velocity by the plane's underbody. The supersonic airflow heated to 4,000 degrees F by the plane's forward motion will be responsible for igniting the hydrogen fuel.

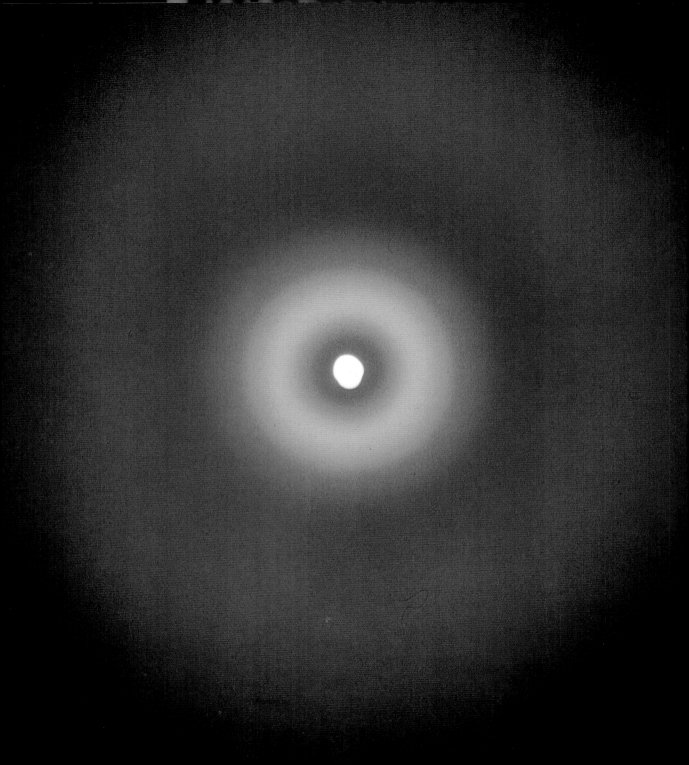

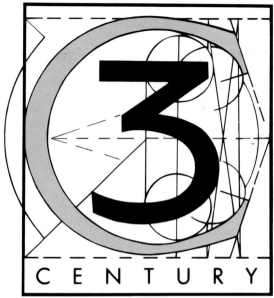

3
C E N T U R Y

2200-2300

THE
MIRACLES
AND
MAGIC
OF
POWER

A new science gives birth to unknown revelations. One world, one people with one power, and the power is the heart. It identifies a true sixth sense, and we may see Machines that Feel, Astral and Instant travel, with more magic than can be imagined.

	MAN-SCIENCE	COMMUNICATIONS	TRANS-PORTATION	MACHIN-ATIONS	ASTRO-NOMICS
2200 · 2210		**THE SIXTH SENSE** The understanding of awareness.		**MANSIDE** What does man have that machines cannot duplicate?	
2210 · 2220			**ASTRAL AND INSTANT TRAVEL** Flying beyond A to B.		**CONTACTING OTHER SPECIES** Joining the galactic community
2220 · 2230			**THE GRID-LOCK** Tying up the loose ends of ground travel.		
2230 · 2240	**THE FEMALE INFLUENCE** How woman's power finds the witch.			**MACHINES THAT FEEL** Emotions on chip - the ultimate computers.	
2240 · 2250	**SENSUOLOGY** Getting into the physical.				
2250 · 2260		**REVELATIONS** Astonishing new ways to talk.	**ALERT VEHICLES** The coming of the AGV.		
2260 · 2270	**SEX AND THE HEART** Moving into new ways of sexuality.				
2270 · 2280					
2280 · 2290		**THE NEW SILENCE** EsP - Extra sensitive Perception.			**FOLDING SPACE** The beginnings of practical Bohm.
2290 · 2300	**MEMORY DESIGN** Finding the cosmic memory.				

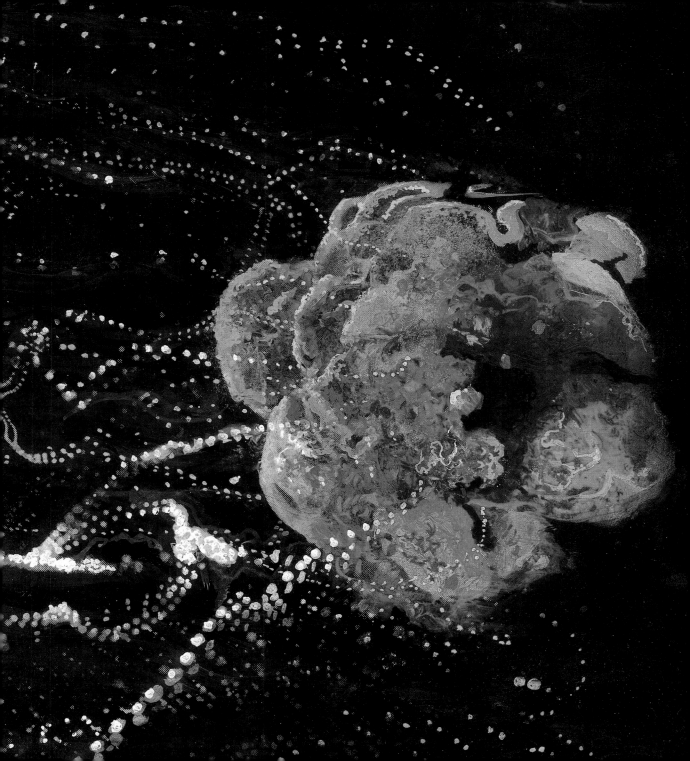

Age of the Heart

2200 • EXTRA SENSITIVE

Once it was ESP — a sort of mind-wave function, but soon it will become EsP — Extra sensitive Perception. Simply a knowledge of the surrounding universe

2230 • AWARENESS

How many senses do we really have? Is it eleven or simply only one? Understanding of the sixth sense brings us to awareness

2250 • NO TRAFFIC JAMS

You simply push the button and it takes you where you want to go No accidents, no wrong turns, no traffic jams

2290 • "DUNE" UNFOLDED

In the movie *Dune* space travelers went by "fold"

SEX
AND THE HEART

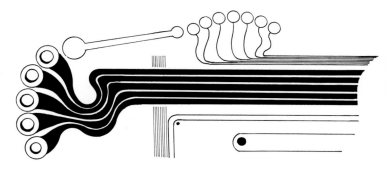

IN THIS THIRD CENTURY of the next millennium we begin to see some true revelations. As woman becomes an increasing power, so the heart steers the human race into different ways of seeing. In the original, very earliest days of Tantric saints, the initiates underwent a sexual ritual which had to be experienced with a female "power holder", a woman, usually from the lower Indian castes, who gave the power of her female sexuality to the man who would then travel the path to enlightenment. But the "power-holder" was always a woman and it was only later that the male-oriented traditional religions such as Hinduism and Buddhism moved away from woman as the initiator of power.

With the return of the female essence and that of the heart, life will travel down the avenue of the female "power-holder" once again.

Revelations are already being strongly felt in the scientific world where, by the third century, we will be facing what might be called "Nonscience", the study of Super-subjectivity, the death of traditional medicine, the acceptance of life as boundless, foundationless and silent, a new kind of silence that could bring us to the brink of a waking dream. The realization that the observer actually creates the observed will bring science effectively to a stand-still — a kind of dead end which can lead nowhere. In more practical spheres this will

create some startling results.

How about human telephones? At the Japanese Ministry of Posts and Telecommunications discussions have already begun, during the latter years of the 1980s to explore the possibility for *ESP-talk* or silent communication. It is expected that before too long we will be able to make our conversations

with one another without picking up a telephone.

Gravity waves are another area of interest. These gravity patterns are thought to travel almost infinite distances and may be used to link humans across the galaxy. The use, also of sub-atomic particles, if they are found to be anything more than probabilities, could be seen, perhaps as carrying particles for communication systems. Sub-atomic particles can travel any distance, through any substance at the speed of light so that communication would be instant and without restrictions.

Of course such devices would naturally also work on the negative side with possible court room clairvoyance. Mind readers would probe witnesses, jurors and judges to check out a case in advance and even figure out who was hiding what. In the criminal world, with mind reading techniques available, there would undoubtedly be a hey-day.

Communication through silence might have

constantly growing advantages. First we would not be clogging up the airwaves with our constant chatter and we could begin to discover how the minds and lives of animals work — discuss the time of day with our plants and flowers and grow like a tree!

But out of all this heightened sensitivity will arise something still more extraordinary — a new sensitivity to sexuality. Life in the mind has given birth to pornography, violence and dissatisfaction — to venereal disease and to AIDS. Life in the Age of the Heart will bring us back to the Eastern ways — to Tantric and Taoist practices and a stronger, softer approach to sex. With a deeper and more sensual approach to relationships. Family planning will take on a new meaning. In order to preserve the chances of a child to grow in the ideal way, parents will not be permitted to have children unless they are able to satisfy certain requirements — financially, home environmental conditions, psychologically and in terms of their health. These conditions are already applied to parents who adopt children — why should the natural birth of a child be any different?

Mothers who are pregnant will be of primary importance in all matters of the home, love, sex, health and well-being. Men will learn to take second place in favor of what will be regarded as a holy state of child-bearing. The creation of life itself will be of the highest religious order giving women back the power and position that they lost thousands of years ago.

Monogamous relationships will not be bound by the laws of marriage as it will be realized that such a powerful and personal emotional state as love cannot be bound by rules. The primary consideration will be a fruitful and happy pairing between two people. With a greater understanding of love and intimacy and a new kind of sexual relating, jealousy and insecurity within relationships will diminish. Such forms of relationship will then permit couples to rise to higher levels of consciousness and general happiness for they will no longer be restricted by mundane jobs, poverty, over-work and poor living conditions. With greater leisure and peace of mind there will be more room for the individual to reach for greater spiritual awareness. And with this the relationships and life-styles will achieve still greater enlightenment. The process might be called a benevolent spiral.

The state of marriage will cease to be of importance. Family formations will occur but will be based on personal confidence and security and not a social or legal order. The relation-ship between marriage and organized religion will also lose its power as religiousness will exist within the individual and have nothing whatever to do with moral laws.

It will become clear that the concept of morality itself is outdated and has only to do with the convenience of the social structure. This convenience will become outmoded and eventually die from lack of use. Personal attitudes and morals will take a totally new form; that of global awareness, personal well-being, individuality and the acceptance of self as God.

Mutual care between all members of the planet and a constant consideration of sharing the same global space will be the greatest transforming factor in the history and evolution of human nature.

REVELATIONS
FROM
THE NEW
SILENCE

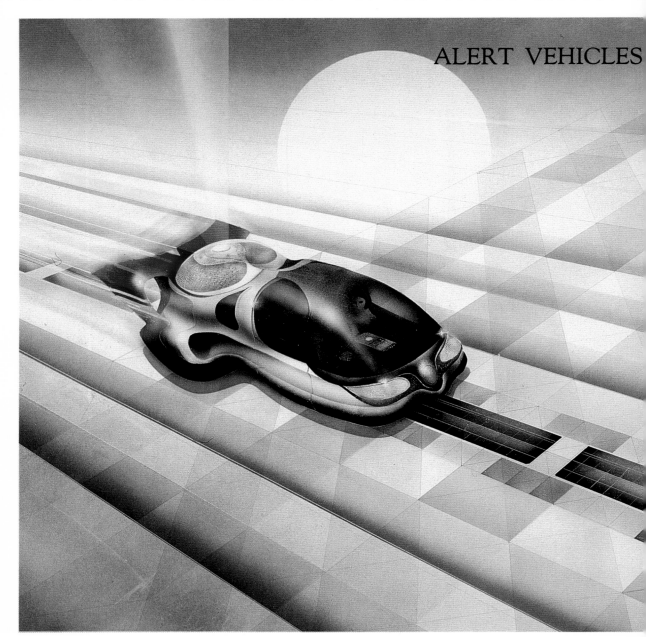

ALERT VEHICLES

AND THE SIXTH SENSE

THE CONCEPT OF "WHOLENESS" proposed by David Bohm in the 20th century has become predominant by the beginning of the 23rd century. The continued process of discovery has led to the gradual revelation that a life which before seemed solid is in fact shadowy. We believe in the 20th century that we are moving from uncertainty to certainty, from sand to clay, whereas the actual understanding will reveal something quite different.

But within this shadow there will perhaps evolve the complete pattern of the universe and it will be available to those who understand its code not because they are able to see it, or observe it, but because they *become* it.

Such a giant paradigm shift will, of course, affect everything and our view of the future must take this into account, even in relation to *Alert Vehicles and the Sixth Sense.*

By the early 21st century General Motors and other car manufacturers will have developed, for commercial transport, a breed of private car which will in effect have a mind of its own. There are already plans on the drawing board for a vehicle with integrated electronic nervous systems and a central brain that will monitor the smallest engine problem, tire skid and spin. The computerized control system will start the car on cold mornings prior to the arrival of the driver, automatically lock or unlock the doors, adjust radio, seats and steering wheel and even scan the forward direction during driving for hidden hazards and enhance vision at night or in foggy weather. The dash will display infrared

images of the road with distance calculations to vehicles ahead related to break control.

The engine will remain, for the beginning of the 21st century, a four-stroke internal combustion engine but the parts will be made from ceramics and metal alloys with computerized fuel injection. All engine functions will be computer monitored, including suspension. But such a vehicle is not so far removed from the present day and far greater jumps will have been taken by the 23rd century. The main feature of computer controlled vehicles is the luxury that will derive (or drive) from the automatically guided vehicle (AGV) or the *Alert Vehicle.* Such a machine will have an immensely complex computer drive system by comparison with today's standards but, as we will see in other chapters, the future's computerization will be dramatically more complex in all facets, given the likely technological advancement in three hundred years from now. Together with, of course, the new science of "wholeness" and the "sixth sense".

The AGV will do everything by subliminal, intro-cerebral contact with the drive-passenger. Computers using digital control systems will operate the vehicle in terms of maneuver and connection with a gridlock system of highways, which of course will require international administrative initiative. Without highway and road control systems the vehicle would not be able to "relate" to the environment and could not therefore drive safely. The drive-passenger would simply take his or her seat and instruct by sub-thought or sixth sense message the destination, time of arrival and preferred route. The AGV would then take over and travel at any speed required from 20 mph to as high as 250 mph to the arrival point. Windscreen and side windows would provide panoramic views or convert either to shaded glass using liquid crystal devices or screens for all round movies,

photo displays or replay of previous journeys recorded in the machine's memory. Inside, the vehicle could be any size and contain all the luxuries and pleasures of home without steering wheel, pedals or gear shift, of course. TV screens will adapt from the plasticated light sensitive side shields with video-phone, entertainment and even holographic image projection. Contact will be possible anywhere in the inhabited galaxy from a tiny receptor on the roof of the vehicle. Power sources for the whole operation of this entirely futuristic machine will almost certainly derive from the sun.

The operation of sixth-sense contact with computers is something practical which should

arise out of the 20th century theorizing on the "oneness" of existence. Today such concepts are way beyond most people's comprehension but within the intervening centuries great jumps will be taken to bring our connection with everything around us into normal everyday practical life.

The ability to cognize a receptive bio-computer network will be a fundamental necessity of the next millennium. We will not speak to computers, we will, in effect, *become* computers. But this should not be perceived as some science fiction imagining for it does not presume that human beings will be walking about the planet looking like the androids from "I Robot". Humans will remain humans and computers computers, but with a natural ability to empathize with everything in our environment, one of the most obvious everyday uses will be the machine contact that will come from human knowledge of how "machine" is. The machine will of course be bio-interfaced, with much of the technological hardware becoming very soft ware — made up of human synapse and human sensory systems, sensitively tuned to receive human communication by the new methods of *multiple-sense contact.*

With more and more sophisticated comprehension of the sense organs and their functions we should be able to bring all the features and talents of our biological organs into harmonized play. Such sense-itivity will seemingly then give us new ways of communicating with everything around us.

Imagine life without traffic jams, eating a sumptuous breakfast aboard your AGV in the morning, on your way to a sub-Earth Maglev train which will take you from New York City Grand Central Station to Bombay in 52 minutes! Multi-level highways and automatic gridlock traffic control systems will provide unhindered travel anywhere, even beneath the oceans. Road accidents will have been eradicated.

MEMORY DESIGN

AT THE CLOSE OF THE 1980s a senior research scientist at Carnegie Mellon University in the USA, named Scott Fahlman, was already working, in common with other scientists — physicists, psychologists, biologists and computer engineers — to create a completely new breed of computer technology. Such researchers have already been given a group name — "Connectionists" and their specific direction is connections with the brain. The standard computer designs have been dropped in this realm of science, in preference to brain-copy computers. Of course, at the end of the 1980s the technologists don't actually know how the brain works, but they know how they *think* it works and so they are basing their intentions on this knowledge.

The intention is to operate computers by the neuron and synapse system with thousands of linking connections between hundreds of units. The method is known as "neural networking" and the early results have been dramatic, with systems adapting to change, learning from changes and absorbing experiences. Before too long the same devices will comprehend speech and talk to operators in all languages and accents and even contain facial recognition capabilities. Of course, the armed forces are the first ones to get in on this new act and no

doubt they will put the innovations of science to some disastrous effect but along the way the main issue is that in order to operate such potentially intelligent devices at their best, the Connectionists must learn more about the "wetware" of the brain itself.

"If the brain were so simple that we could understand it, we would be so simple that we couldn't." So said Emerson Pugh and there may be much in this simple judgment for the brain is a daunting "machine" to try to copy with systems that literally alter as you watch them, giving out new signals and methods with each experiment. There may be as many as one hundred billion neurons in the brain, and each of these is connected with thousands of other neurons. A high level neuron cell such as a *Purkinje* cell can contain a hundred thousand synapses transmitting signals, and a single thought probably engenders an incredible number of calculations all at the same time, with vast groups of neurons all working together to arrive at the result.

Developing theory also indicates that memory and information systems within the brain are connected to outside stimuli like a kind of cosmic thought-field, with material flooding into the reception areas of the body from endless and spaceless sources so that each

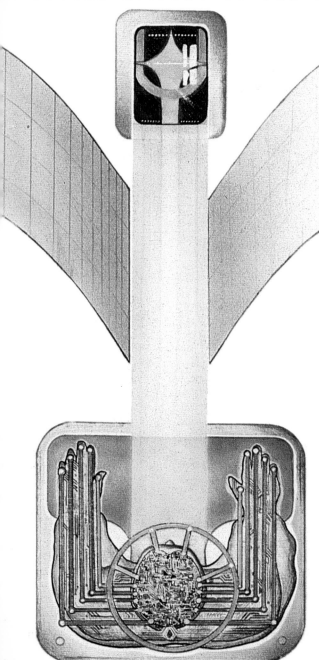

thought pattern of memory is drawn, not from a library of recorded information within the brain but as a kind of replication from a form of *Akashic* memory field. (The Akashic Records were said, by the Theosophists, to be universal records of life, past, present and future.)

Any computer which hoped to operate along the same lines as the brain would therefore need a reception center several times the size of the largest space-receiving saucer presently in the world!

But of course the purpose of building computers that operate like the brain is not to be *like* the brain. It is to be more efficient and effective so the original intention of creating computers in ways that we *think* the brain works is perhaps more practical. If this line of development continues into the 23rd century we shall be looking at machines that feel and have

memory capabilities that can literally be designed to work for anything specific such as space vehicles, ground vehicles, and even for individual human problems or ailments.

Such systems would have totally different programming features to the present genre of computer which requires an operator to "feed" information into the system in some computer language. The computer then operates exclusively and only on this information and if there is no reference, there is no answer to an input problem.

The synapse-type computer being developed by the Connectionists *learns* how to know about something. It will be given, for example, a selection of information that it will scan until it is familiar with the content and then make comparisons between different sets of information, for example between different animal types so that it effectively "knows" one animal from another. It will then be capable of making further deductions from this kind of information and eventually will be able to build new information of its own.

One of the ultimate developments from such a system will, of course, be the computer's ability to repair and improve itself — to grow!

An old story was once told by a science fiction writer of a group of scientists who decided to build the ultimate computer. In

Machines That Feel

order to make the computer the biggest and best ever to have been constructed they fed it with every available piece of information in the known universe. Their final desire was to ask the computer an "ultimate" question and once the machine was completed it stood several blocks wide and higher than any high rise building in New York. Once satisfied of its complete "education" the scientists asked the question — "Who is God?" The Answer came from the depths of the vast computer — "I am."!

In our experimentation and future growth it is evidently more and more that we look to replicate ourselves in order to discover exactly what we can do. We build computers, communications, transport forms and genetic capabilities in order to understand the way we are — like mirrors of the human power in the world where we are largely in shadow as to the truth of our nature.

If all this science and technology is going to result in an awareness of God — or the God in us all, then by the 23rd century we may have reached some extraordinary conclusions. With computers and other machines that are capable of feeling, memory and mind designs that can be formulated in any fashion we wish, perhaps the result will be an Earth technology of such complexity that it can operate only through its own understanding of itself. Man will delegate the process of science to mechanisms that are cleverer than ever man can be. Or perhaps there is also another way.

Most of the large scale discoveries that mankind has come across have arrived as if from nowhere and then been translated into mathematical or physical terms. Einstein was known to state that his most expansive theories occurred as though in a flash of light — without any reasoning behind them and the process of proving the flash of inspiration was back tracking from the conclusion to a logical theory in reverse. If we remember our billions of synapses and neurons flashing and

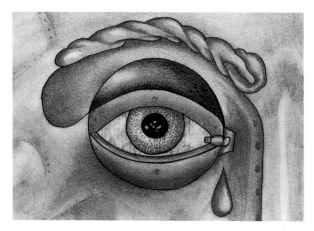

communicating with thousands of fields of other neurons — imagine the inspiration of Albert Einstein! How many billions of neurons were needed to come to his awe inspiring conclusions? Perhaps a computer will be built that can rush through logic and come to instinctive conclusions in this same fashion. Perhaps mankind will reach a point where he can put the work of science and technology into the hands of machines. In this case, there would be no purpose in understanding the logical aspect of any of the great discoveries, for they would be made by computers. The results would simply be accepted and applied — by the computers!

Given enough time and additional rapid advances, the computer would — as we have been warned by scientists and science fiction writers — end up ruling the world we live in, the human being could never keep pace.

But ultimately the success or failure of such a computer direction would rest on one factor. If the new directions and networks set up *do* ape the human functions then they may well serve to help us be those "simple" people who can understand our own brains. If they go in other directions and into the bargain leave us standing, God in a chip might not be such good news.

ASTRAL AND INSTANT TRAVEL

UNDER THE NEWEST UNDERSTANDING of nature which is, we predict, likely to be the format of the 23rd century, everything in life and the universe is enfolded in and enfolds the whole; parts are only relative parts — and are in fact our abstractions only (and these abstractions are also enfolded into the whole). Out of this way of considering the universe we might suppose that this wholeness can create, or unfold, within itself, anything it wishes. It happens to have unfolded us, humans. It might just as easily unfold anything else living and such life would be quite as suitable to the universe as an occupant of it, as we are. But it might be very different also — so different in fact that we could not even see, hear, touch, or sense it in the least. There are scientists, for example Nicholas Rescher a philosopher of science at the University of Pittsburgh and Marvin Minsky, the world's foremost computer expert, who believe that we may be able to communicate with extra-terrestrial life through the basic reasoning of computer arithmetic.

A very basic computer has been built,

named the Turing machine, that it is believed may be used to communicate with any alien life on the basis that, even though the physiological structure is different, the mind will inevitably be the same as our. How scientists have reached this conclusion is uncertain, as mental reasoning would seem to be as dependent on environment as physical appearance, and physical formation would also appear to be somewhat influenced by the shape of the mind.

The investigations in question apply the abstraction of mathematics and its attendant physical science, on a wide research area, to discover *all* the possible languages that would be usable by alien species. There is no question as to whether such a human abstraction as mathematics could apply in the first place to a species of creatures who were not remotely human.

With the new awareness of universal wholeness it would seem much more likely that communication would take place on levels that we are today unable to tap. These channels of contact might be closer to the science fiction stories foretold in such series as *The Twilight Zone* than those envisaged by regular dualistic science. Sub-vocal levels of communication such

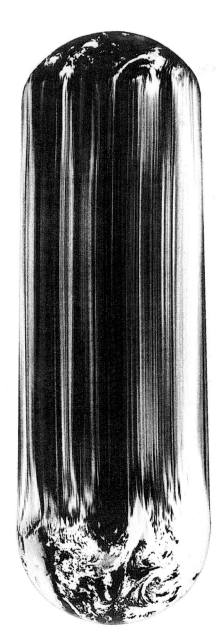

as what is now known as ESP might turn out to be more effective than any languages could be. Contact from brain to brain or body to body needs no verbal or written language and relies instead on reality and not abstraction.

Extra Sensory Perception by the 23rd century is likely to be changed to Extra *Sensitive* Perception, when more subtle senses are discovered within the human frame, and this new form of *EsP* might be our most effective link, not only with one another but also with alien presences. In fact some would say, especially those who study UFOs, that such aliens are already amongst us but because our senses are either not subtle enough or because they simply exist in our unconscious, we are unable to know of these presences.

Another likely future form of contact is that of instant and/or astral travel.

There are alpha wave bio-feedback machines being developed in the 1990s that include an "astral travel" button. Push the button and the alpha wave rhythm can simulate the conditions in the body and brain that potentially send us out of our bodies. We can thereby travel to any distance and at any time, at will. The only problem that may be envisaged is letting go of the button! Some convincing stories have been told by those who have had access to these prototype machines — visiting friends and noting what book they are reading, pushing the button on the machine to come home and then calling up and verifying the truth. But who knows.

A more likely area of development is into instant travel on a molecular transfer level.

Here again we return for the umpteenth time to the concept of wholeness, into which everything seems to fit.

If the universe is made up of enfolded entity, everything being contained and enfolded within that enfoldment, then the transfer of one abstraction — a human being — into the enfolded universe and then out of it again on the other side of the Atlantic, might not be so tricky. Bohm's theories insist that we are all made up like droplets from the whole ocean and yet are contained in that ocean at all time and space. What follows most logically, or illogically if you prefer, is that the droplet of humanity in one of its individual forms could easily be drawn up again into that enfolded reality to be unfolded again — either in the same form elsewhere or even in a different form right here.

In the movie "Dune", one of the concepts

borrowed from Bohm's theories was that of "Folding through space". The flight captains of the future were depicted as rather ugly characters who became connected with the universe through the constant ingestion of a particular drug and once past some four thousand years or so of this heavy trip, they became able to fold space, giving instant travel anywhere in the universe. Science fiction or not, this concept fits perfectly with Bohm's theories of space and time being here and now. It also fits pretty snugly with much of the Eastern flavor of philosophy which has been telling us for over twenty-five centuries that there is no question of space being out there or time being past and future. All space is right in every molecule and atom and quark of your and my body, the air we breath and the food we eat.

News from another star

All time is centered in the now. And this space/time un-continuum is enfolded everywhere rather like the holographic plate.

We happen to have unfolded it into the present shape it's in — not always so great — but we could just as easily unfold it into a totally different shape — using it also for our instant trip to Mars, Jupiter and beyond.

Such a concept has its astonishing implications and means that for all of this century we have been barking up entirely the wrong tree. The progress of science in the 20th century may look to the 23rd century roughly how the science of leeches from the 16th century looks to us today.

But isn't that always the case? It is only we here, doing our very best, who view that *as* the best.

The science of rockets and propulsion could well be as archaic by the 23rd century as the "penny farthing."

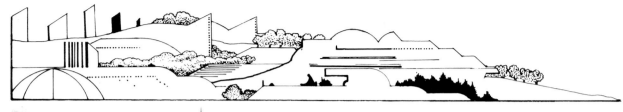

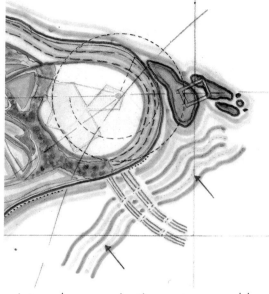

Internal communication systems would operate through cellular units connected by short-wave radio to satellite stations and the unit would have an auto-banking provision within the computer for financial transfers, directly connected to the personal or corporate account.

There would be no fuel costs, a self-maintaining hardware system operated by the "synapse" type computers mentioned in the last century and a recycling plant engineered into the kitchen.

Such methods can also be expanded into larger living and also commercial buildings, though perhaps not so easily including the moveability aspect.

Large condominiums operated in the above

principles could be feasible much earlier than the 24th century and warehouses and office buildings can already be constructed that save as much as 70% of fuel bills by solar operation for power units.

Power sources on a city scale are likely to be supplied from beneath the ground as well as above the sky. Hot Rock wells will be buried deep into sub-city areas with water pumped down into cracks in the rocks which will heat it and then store it in vast reservoirs which can then be circulated from for large areas of central heating or power provision. Rocks don't lose their heat and the only cost will be the initial wells and the circulation of the water, the power for which can be provided by the Hot Rock wells. This is already getting close to perpetual motion!

Those who remain on this planet will, almost certainly, find themselves in Aqua-cities. If population increases even at half its present rate and if even half of that resulting population remains on Earth there will no longer be a lot of room left on land — with some 80 billion humans in occupation. Given workable sub-marine development, there is much more space beneath the sea than above it.

A Frenchman named Jacques Rougerie, living

Such aqua-cities would be ideal areas for communal living and multi-parent families that are likely to be operating at this time would be largely independent of surface communities though of course still governed by the same laws and conditions.

It is even considered possible, that given enough time in under water conditions, mankind may develop greater natural abilities suitable to this habitat. Rougerie is a member of a world wide organization who see a future sub-species of man they have named

AQUA-CITIES

Already on the drawing board — aqua-cities that change man's physical nature

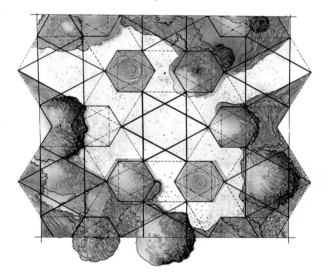

in a large houseboat on the River Seine in Paris, has already begun the process of working out how aqua-cities could be built and enjoyed.

An underwater village would be built largely of concrete resin molding, anchored to the sea bed by steel cables. Local farming would be for kelp or edible sea weeds and travel between separate areas of the village or city would happen along tubular, water-filled streets along which the residents would swim!

In order to avoid microbic dirt or infection, special ultraviolet light baths would be in all home and work areas, and antiseptic showers would be taken daily. Of course, the largest proportion of the underwater occupants would be fish which would be farmed and developed in vast quantity.

Air to the under water cities would be provided by artificial gills built into the structures and power for heating would operate from special "geothermal" generators that operate on the changes of temperature inherent in the ocean itself.

"amphibious man." And, in order to test his theories and vision, he and other experimenters have built and lived in sub-aqua modules for a month at a time.

Another development in sea culture has literally grown out of the innovation of a German-born architect named Wolf Hilbertz who discovered that it is possible to "acrete" a durable building material by passing an electric current through wire. The resulting accretion, named "Seacrete", is now being "grown" into the first major sized building in Galveston Bay , Texas.

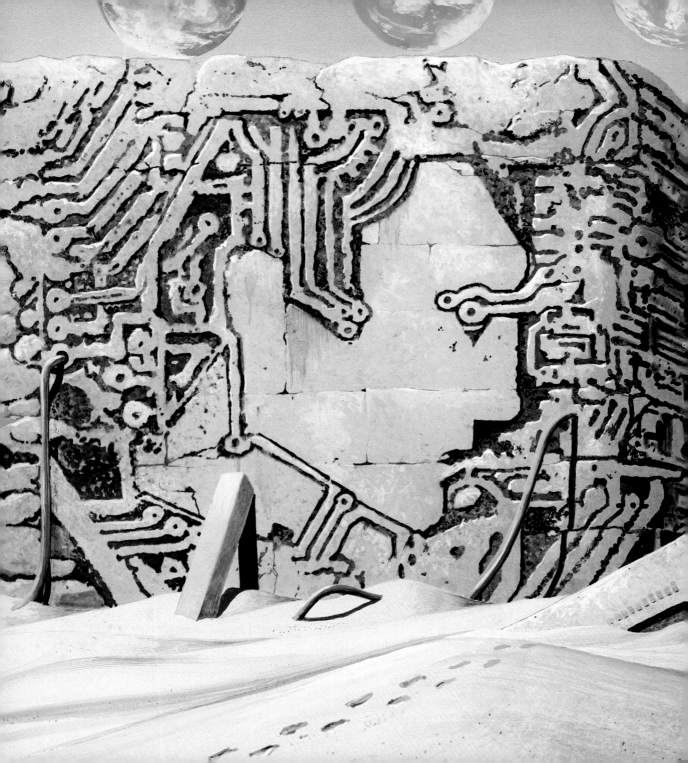

POWER
OF
THE
PAST

IF WE LOOK BACK INTO OUR own past today, there is still, for periods prior to the beginning of this century, only a limited amount of recorded material. Movies and photographs really only began to be available at the end of the 19th century, so that our view of the past is necessarily patchy and often relates only to special events like personalities and feature movies.

But during this century and the coming years there is such a wealth of both private and public material on record that by the 24th century it will be possible to sample the past with a large degree of accuracy. We will know the flavor of the past in the future.

The time may come too, before the 24th century, when holographic records and computer enhanced information will fill in many of the gaps and with the coming likelihood of machines that feel, even the emotions and attitudes of today will be available to our descendants.

Libraries of visually recorded information are already in existence and mankind's passion for the past will surely result in vast computerized libraries recording every moment of time.

Perhaps therefore we shall see a new science named *The Archaeology of Time* which will use past experience to plan future changes somewhat like the ancient Theosophical *Akashic Records* that were believed to contain records of all events, past, present and future in one giant library.

But here we come across a change that is predicted in the concept of time travel itself, for scientists such as Ilya Prigogine and David Bohm have begun a journey down new avenues of time appreciation. They state that time is not a temporal affair but exists at all times in the present. That we unfold time in the present and that all future and past events exist right here and now. It is only a matter of tapping into the present to see the rest of life's span.

We might therefore suppose that one of the likely careers to flourish in a time when time is accessible, will be *Time Technicians* whose task will be to investigate the possibilities of time manipulation — if manipulation is to be the method.

One of the most popular central issues of science fiction is time travel stories in which our hero travels back into the past and alters some aspect of it only to find himself dead in his own time. Time technology, in this linear sense, however, does not seem to be the way of the future (which is incidentally already a misnomer as our own journey into the future during this book is likely to prove unlikely once we discover how time is really related to life).

Time Technicians would presumably have particular interests — for example those of references from the past or trends for the future and these might no longer be of interest if we discover, as has already been indicated, that evolution does not unfold in an experiential learning process but simply changes and then moves off in a different direction. It is only our minds that demand there should be a progressive factor to life.

Time Technicians might therefore be more interested in the limits of time — infinity, black

(or gray) holes, time changes in terms of how a gad fly will live a whole life-time while a human only passes a day. There is much evidence today that points towards entirely different time scales for different events. For example, most of us will have experienced the speed at which time passes when events demand deep concentration and how slow it passes when there is nothing to do. These events are being thought now to be quite different time scales, and those around us are actually operating in these varying dimensions all the time. Our minds retain a linear factor, and some continuity by keeping clocks that tick at the same rate and seasons, weeks, days and months, but these things are all man-made and may not have the slightest thing to do with "natural time" spans.

The river of life *flows*, after all, and within such flows there are constant changes — both in space, matter and especially time.

David Bohm, one of today's most gifted theoretical physicists, regards time as something different from the classical physicists who have always viewed it as a primary dimension alongside space and matter. Bohm says that time is secondary and arises out of the unfolding of a higher reality. This can be more

ARCHAEOLOGY OF TIME

easily appreciated by remembering those experiences where you have been long parted from a friend and yet when you meet again it seems as though no time has passed. It might, in this case, be considered that perhaps you and the friend have been operating on a like time scale which is different from those scales in the lives of others.

In a radio-active atom a previously inert nucleus may suddenly emit a particle after a second, a month or several years and there may be no way of predicting the rate of the emissions. Clearly, in such cases, the atomic nucleus is operating on its own time.

For the Time Technician, therefore, the study of time would be more involved in the ways in which time unfolds from the greater whole of the universe. He would be concerned to find practical uses for this knowledge, such as methods of improving people's lives so that they occupied their own time zones and lived by their own time rates. This could in the event, have a lot to do with the instance of disease and unhappiness or mental sicknesses of the future, for if we learn to fulfill our lives according to our own unfolding of time, they might turn out to be less stressed and urgent.

DEATH OF MEDICINE

MEDICINE, DRUGS, BIOLOGY and everything connected with the human condition will come under severe investigation during the years between now and the 24th century. We have already looked closely at the revolutionary new concepts concerned with physics and the new view of universal science and these same aspects of the wholeness of existence must inevitably touch biology and medicine also. The following resume will bring us up to date with the more advanced forms of medicine likely to be in existence during the 24th century.

Medical advances, coupled with changed behavioral and nutritional patterns, are likely to imply substantial increases in life expectancy (particularly amongst 50s age groups) in developed countries.

Genuine cures or very effective treatment of broad classes of cancer will be available — together with a much improved understanding of the interaction of genetic, environmental and behavioral factors in the causes of cancer.

Drugs will become available to cure or ameliorate allergies, anxiety, asthma, auto-immune diseases, caries, depression, hypertension, some mental illnesses and

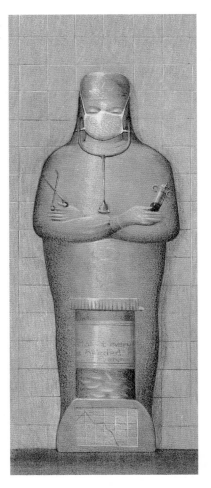

neurological disorders, obesity, senility, sexual dysfunction and thrombosis.

Effective artificial hearts and kidneys are likely to be available, as well as effective vaccines against most forms of viral diseases.

The deaf and blind will be aided by electronic devices which convert audio and visual signals into forms that can be interpreted. Cures for certain types of deafness and blindness will become available. Expanded computers will be used to advise on diagnosis and medical treatment. For example, the following story might soon become a reality — "Mrs Jones has had a low-back pain for several weeks which bed rest and aspirin have not helped. She consults her family doctor in the city to which she has recently moved and explains that the pain started soon after playing tennis. His examination reveals limitation of movement in the elbow and tenderness in the back.

The doctor consults his P.C., which has access to a nationwide computer network. He links to the hospital computer in the city which Mrs. Jones moved from. This hospital has electronic medical records, to which authorized persons may gain access with the patient's permission, and within seconds the doctor finds that Mrs.

Jones had a lumpectomy to remove a small tumor of the breast five years ago. Mrs. Jones had neglected to mention this.

The doctor disconnects the network and consults QMR, a diagnosing system which has knowledge of over six hundred diseases, and suggests that Mrs. Jones may have arthritis, muscle strain or a recurrence of the cancer. The doctor is reassured to see the QMR's second opinion agrees with his concern and orders a bone scan to eliminate the possibility of the recurrence of cancer."

Chemical control of some aspects of human aging will be available. We might eventually use hormones to bolster our immune systems, virus-like vaccines to slow the death of cells, and uric acid to prevent the destruction of our genes. Such supplements could help us maintain our health and vigor throughout much of our life span of 115 years. What's more, in the 24th century these otions will be dwarfed by a new, more potent generation of "longevity pill". Enzyme drinks will endow us with the ability to repair each new nick in our armor of DNA, and synthetic neurohormones will literally reset the aging clock in our brains. Instead of simply keeping us healthier longer, these new drugs will push the outside of the aging envelope,

MEDICINE INNOVATIONS

eventually increasing our life-span by dozens of years.

Nerve cells "talk" to one another in the brain through electrical signals that generate a weak magnetic field, about one billionth the strength of the earth's. Now surgeons and brain researchers can monitor magnetic patterns emerging from the human brain with a new computer-based technology called magnetoencephalography (MEG). The subject either lies down on a bed or sits in a chair. A complicated electrical device, known as a neuromagnetometer, is placed near the subject's head. It acts as an antenna and picks up the magnetic fields emerging from the brain. It senses magnetic-field patterns produced by brain cells, locates the field's source, and takes a snapshot every millisecond.

Parkinson's disease, chronic pain, manic depression, and schizophrenia could be diagnosed more precisely and thus treated more effectively. People may revive from comas more quickly if stimulated, but finding what stimulus works best with a particular person — light, sound, touch — presents a problem. With a good brain map and MEG, doctors will quickly determine which stimuli reach the brain and then go on to select appropriate treatment.

Medical Materials

New polymers, ceramics, glasses and composites are among the many materials now enabling medical engineers to design innovative, and increasingly biocompatible, replacements for damaged human tissues. Biomaterials lend themselves to an array of applications, from intraocular-lens replacements to artificial hearts. To be acceptable as a biomaterial a substance must certainly pass mechanical muster, but it also has to be biocompatible: it must interact with the host in a non toxic, controlled and predictable way. Inertness is an important

their initial purpose. The normal heart beats approximately 40 million times each year. Artificial parts must therefore be made of materials that are able to remain flexible without tearing or becoming misshapen. Whereas most materials for cardiovascular systems have to be elastic and blood-compatible, materials for osseous, or bone, implants must be rigid and stress resistant. Metallic prostheses have long been the mainstay of both orthopedics and dentistry. They are mechanically and compositionally quite different from a host's tissues. In the hope of increasing the life of implants, over the past 15 years there has been considerable

objective for many purposes, however workers now recognize that not all interactions between foreign materials and the body are bad.

Several materials that are highly interactive are proving to be increasingly valuable. Some implant materials form chemical bonds with nearby tissue, stabilizing the implant. Certain other materials are gradually reabsorbed by the body when they are no longer needed for

experimentation using bone replacements made of inert non-metallic materials, for instance polymers reinforced with strong carbon fibers. Various laboratories have also developed "bioactive" (interactive) ceramics, glasses and glass-ceramics that form chemical bonds at their surfaces with adjacent bone and are believed to encourage new bone to form. A biodegradable skin substitute has been developed, called Stage 1 skin, that appears to stimulate new skin growth. The future is sure to see increasingly complex uses of composites and bioactive and biodegradable materials.

Body-Repair Shop

Developments into new kinds of computer microchips that can be implanted in the body to repair or replace the lost functions of damaged nerves, will have transformed body-part surgery well before the 24th century.

Human trials for devices like artificial ears or simulators to control paralyzed limbs could begin within the next ten years; practical implants might be in use within 15 years.

the job, so instead as many as forty microscopic gold wires, emanating from the chip, press up against the surface of a single nerve cell. The more wires on a chip the better the communication between brain and cell.

Computer scientist Morton Grosser and neurologist Joseph Rosen at Stanford University plan to build a tiny integrated circuit that will function like a telephone switchboard. In use the "switchboard" would be implanted between the two halves of a severed nerve. After several weeks the nerve fibers would grow into each end of the unit. Then the researchers would identify, using a computer, which parts of the nerve on each side of the cut

So far doctors are unable to find a way past damaged nerves to restore lost functions even though the brain remains capable of sending a nerve impulse. This is where the new microchips come in. For good control or clear senses, a prosthesis needs to communicate with many nerve cells just as the brain does. But like the brain it must talk to one nerve cell at a time, otherwise noise from other cells will drown the message. Ordinary wires are much too big for

were originally part of each nerve fiber. Once this is accomplished they would use the switchboard to link up the appropriate fibers so that nerve impulses would once again flow down the fiber. In theory this should restore normal control over a limb.

These are just a few of the innovations that will become normal medical practice in the next three hundred years.

DNA AND MEMORY THAT NEVER FORGETS

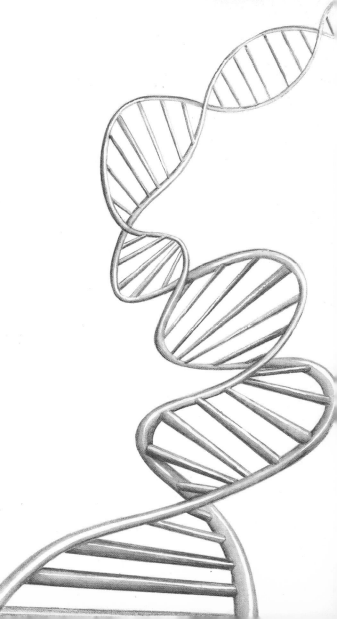

A PAPER PUBLISHED IN the scientific journal "Nature" in September 1988 by John Cairns and two of his colleagues at the Harvard School of Public Health in Boston, put forward the idea that the structure of the body may be able to receive information fed back from the environment in the form of selective memory traces, which are then integrated into the foundations of life — the DNA of the body — which is then, of course, passed on to the next generation. Put another way, we make our own evolution happen.

The attitudes of the 20th century have been that there is someone else out there — or worse still nobody out there — making all this happen (or not making it happen according to the persuasion). This neatly sidesteps the need to be responsible for what is happening, for if it is random and separate we need not feel guilty if we foul it up, for perhaps "Nature" is fouling it up already. If we discover that only *we* are making all this happen, then we have to start figuring out whether what we do is OK and we have also to take responsibility for all our past mistakes.

Such a fundamental idea brings into question many of the concepts of biology as evolutionary development has always been considered in the light of the revelations proposed by Darwin. All such considerations are now in question.

We may see, therefore, during the next millennium, some extraordinary realizations connected to the same theory of wholeness, mentioned several times in this book, supposed by David Bohm.

Evolution for mankind may turn out to be a kind of sub-structure of the whole universal

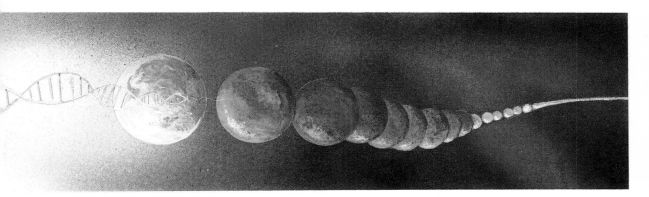

enfoldment. And here again we can expect to see the "morphogenetic field" concept of Rupert Sheldrake in process — that mankind operates within subtle fields of change which work on a universal scale and include human behavior.

The DNA memory concept draws close to these two massive scale potentials in so far as if the human frame is part and parcel of a huge existential activity it would thereby naturally have access to experiential memories around it which would be accessible by all generations of man.

Many satisfactory explanations would result from a combination of such ideas — past life memories, death experiences, where people return from death with particular memories of what it is like after death, deja vu. The whole area of psychic awareness would also find a comfortable place in such a universal theory — for if we are bound together by fields of energy — if the universe is one bounded and extraordinarily complex entity — flowing and changing within itself as one entity, then communication activities such as ESP, kinetic movement and channeling may have some ground in that reality.

We have considered sub-conscious communication until now as a wave band transfer of some kind, which is seen to operate like any of the other wave systems in our conscious environment. But if we consider mankind as one with his environment perhaps there is no need for any wave transfer at all — the knowledge of other people, animals, any stimulating activity around us, is inherent within us all. We have only to learn the method of getting in touch.

The present understanding of evolutionary progress is already showing some unanswerable questions and amongst those proposed by Sheldrake in his new ideas

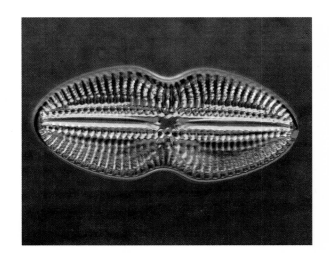

surrounding morphogenetic fields is one concerning "form."

All genetic codes within the cells of the human body are the same. In other words, the DNA structure does not vary from one place to another over the body. So what decides which cell is going to go where? How does a cell that is making up the brain "decide" to form itself as a brain cell? How does a toe-cell decide to be a toe-cell? The form of the DNA is not evident and this provides us with a major gap in the evolutionary process. And yet, we rarely manage to end up, as humans, with our toes in place of our heads — though some would say that a few humans have their brains in their feet!

Sheldrake says, as we have seen in his own essay within the first chapter of this book, that there are hidden forms that mediate between the DNA and the environment of the genetic structure — i.e. man's universe. That these forms work in a flow of activity that fits with man's physiological and energy substance.

Should such a theory be proven, some dramatic changes will create a completely new form of understanding in both the areas concerning DNA and genetics and our view of our own evolution, by the time we reach the 24th century.

Suppose that the DNA does have a constant access to cosmic experiences and that there is a flow of the past happening around us, to which the body, the DNA, if you like, can tap into. This would mean that we could eventually have complete access to our own pasts.

Coupled with the Bohm concept of all time being here and now, we would, through our own natural resources, be able to become clairvoyant and look back into the past of mankind with complete sensual accuracy.

Science would, of course, cast this idea aside as dramatic and off the point and they would, perhaps during the 20th century, be right. But should these now theoretical factors enlarge and grow into realities then within the next few

hundred years we might indeed be able to touch the 20th century, for example, and feel it as it was (is).

We can bring yet another aspect of this forward as a further hypothesis. The Eastern cultures such as India, have formulated the religious concept of reincarnation, which, briefly, implies that we, as spirits, do not die within one lifetime but the spirit or soul carries forward to the next life and enters another body. Each lifetime is a learning process in which growth to higher states of consciousness is achieved.

A more sceintific approach to such a philosophy might be that the morphogenetic fields that adapt and create the forms of life — that provide the experience which tells a human to be a human and an elephant to be an elephant — are created by the constant existence of those forms. And those forms are made up of past lives.

There is much interest in the whole therapeutic concept of past lives, particularly within the West Coast of America, and given a more stable form of making contact with our own past lives, the fashion would surely surge into a powerful reality — even stretching through to a kind of time travel.

 LIVING

PASTS

T HE WHOLE SUBJECT OF past lives has still to be quantified and remains in the latter years of the 20th century a subject largely composed of imagination and religious dogma but it may slowly become more attached to the growing realms of science as we begin to take a more serious interest in the phenomenon of channelling, "after-death" experiences and other psychic phenomena. There is such a wealth of experience, both documented and consistant, surrounding past-life memories that any investigation into these "para" realms will become very revealing in the future.

How do we explain experiences of the sixth sense, childhood memories of birth which contain knowledge of other lives, for example? It may be that many of the modern-day channellers are being discredited but they keep coming back with fresh information which seems accurately related to concrete aspects of provable life.

If the ideas of reincarnation are taken at all seriously we could easily imagine a time when our relationships with the old and long dead are seen more in the light of contact with living memories. Ghosts, for example can be seen clearly as supportive phenomena of the concept of morphogenetic fields. If we leave behind traces of our lives in the form of ghosts, perhaps these are simply the form-fields that Sheldrake speaks of, drifting about without physical manifestation — like time travellers still attached to Earth and yet only visible on a different plain.

WE TOUCHED ON TIME TRAVEL during the earlier part of this century, as a concept that is unfolding in some interesting directions during the last years of the 20th century. So, for the purposes of the closing years of the 24th century, we might look into the more spectacular forms of time travel — verging, as they do, on science fiction. For our purposes, however, we will call the following proposals *Science Faction*.

Suppose for a moment (of *your* time) that all forms of existence remain within the universe in the shape of mixed fields, absorbed and re-absorbed as they fade in and out through history. Dinosaurs, for example, disappeared in their concrete and solid form and became a memory, but this memory remained as matter in the same form as thoughts are matter — if you like, as though floating in energy shapes

TIME TRAVEL

Perhaps the dinosaurs are still with us in invisible form... and time travel merely getting in touch with these form-fields.

within the fabric of existence. All forms, therefore, co-exist and everything which we are now creating, even if it has become extinct by the 24th century, is still mixed in with everything else that "lives" then. The fact that the human only has senses which appear to detect matter, means that the non-matter forms are not visible. But given a greater and more sensitive response mechanism, *all* forms might become available for our awareness. Let us predict that by the 24th century this greater sensitivity is available.

That extraordinarily complex, by our standards, bio-feedback equipment or computerized technological awareness devices are there for us to use.

Picture the average person of the 24th century, seated at home on a windy and rainy afternoon, looking about for something to do to fill the leisure time. Inside her home there is no longer a TV screen but a "Time Monitor" which is in direct touch with morphogenetic field structures within her immediate environment. The TM machine reproduces into a visual event, the time and space factors present in holographic reality within the cell structures of the form fields that are literally floating within her own cells and the cells of the air around her. The computerized and digitized equipment can interpret temporal events into present reality in the form of a four-dimensional abstraction right there in front of her. There is no need for her to achieve this event by tapping into memory banks at a TV studio or by pulling out video tapes that have been pre-recorded from massive Hollywood movie projects costing millions of dollars. The events that she will view are real events reproduced from a universal or cosmic field of substance which derive from the unravelling of information contained in a higher reality — costlessly unique and dramatic and absolutely accurate to the nth degree of some event in the past.

She can, should she wish, tune into the 20th century and view the grand events such as the assassination of John F. Kennedy, as it really happened. She could examine the true assassins, watch them undergo the processes that resulted in the President's death and identify all the characters in this real-life drama.

Alternatively she can look at micro-cosmic events such as the life of a tiny organism within a remote part of India as it's life unfolds in the past. She can watch two people gossiping in Birmingham Alabama or come in direct contact with Picasso as he paints, Nostradamus as he predicts or even the reader of this book as he thumbs through its pages and reads about her watching the reader as he reads about her watching the reader read about her watching the reader etc. etc.

Her connection with the past will be identifiable because it will depend for its interpretation, largely on forms that can be "form-ulated". There will be direct references that can be identified and therefore digitized by the computer system into abstract shapes and forms that are ordered according to modern understanding within that time. Put simply, she will know what she is looking at

because she will remember it — perhaps not directly — but from learned knowledge of the past.

But in terms of the future it might be very different. If the same theories are applied to future events, form-field structures may not exist at all that are necessarily ready to create future events. It may be that these forms only occur out of events which create a critical mass.

A critical mass is something like what happens when we get over-stressed. Perhaps from a day's heavy and stressful work, we eventually collapse from exhaustion. This is a sort of critical mass event because it changes our whole movement and trend, towards something new. Critical mass events can also happen on a major scale such as with the Earth or within the whole universe that we know. The "Big Bang" was a critical mass event.

So it may not be so easy for our friend at home within the 24th century to view the future in as much detail as the past, insofar as the form-fields that would be available to make up the future would only be those that have been formed in the past. The future would therefore look a bit like a jig-saw puzzle with many of its pieces missing or else like a simple repeating series of the past or present.

But, contrary to this, we are still told that the past and the future exist in the present — that they co-exist as a form in a non-linear fashion within an enfolded timelessness. Does this not mean then that we have the future with us now and with or without critical masses we could still see what is to come?

We could trace the form of our remaining lives, the form of our deaths, our children's lives and even the forms of the critical mass events which are to change the forms of the future. And when we reach those future forms and make them into concrete reality we can look back at ourselves looking forward, looking back — through the everlasting mirrors of the universe.

C5

CENTURY

2400-2500

GETTING
AWAY
FROM
IT
ALL

If the universe were formed by fields of energy, like auras around all things, then we would know why we have disease, why we have love, and happiness — and one day we might identify these fear-fields and love-fields and even create them.

	THEO-SCIENCE	ASTRO-NOMICS	PHILO-THINKING	EARTH-NATURE	MAN-SCIENCE
2400 2410		**TIME-JUMPING** Warp-sense confuses time, anti-clock wise.		**MOVING HOUSE** First fabricated planet, a million miles from Earth.	
2410 2420		**FLIGHT AND THE SCRAMJET** A mach 10 flight system out-ramming the Ramjet.			**ANDROIDISM** Androids *do* dream of electric sheep
2420 2430	**MASTERS AND GURUS** Burst of enlightenment, unequalled since late 1980s.		**BENEVOLENT CIRCLE** A new math grown out of positive thinking.		
2430 2440					**CRYOGENICS AND REBIRTH** Cancer cures — re-awaken-ing of the frozen dead.
2440 2450	**THE NEW CONFIDENCE** After confidence comes the Fall.			**RELIGION AND THE HEART** God at home again.	
2450 2460					**ROBOPATHIC LABOR** Nothing left for the human to do.
2460 2470				**TUNNELING THE PLANET** From Bombay to New York in 45 minutes underground.	
2470 2480		**THE GRAY HOLE** New negative space, part matter, part anti-matter.		**THE PERFECT WORLD** Too Good to be True.	
2480 2490	**THE NEW BUDDHA** The Return of Holiness.				
2490 2500		**THE BOUNDED UNIVERSE** Infinity has walls.		**SECOND EARTH** Finding ways of dealing with population.	

The Half Millennium

2450 • ANDROIDS

The near human robot built from bio-tissue will serve mankind — but who will decide the difference between test-tube babies and androids?

2460 • TUNNELING EARTH

It will be possible in this century to walk into Grand Central Station, New York take a train and come up in Bombay 52 minutes later!

2480 • CRYOGENIC REBIRTH

Cryogenics in the 20th century freezes heads in the hope one day of adding new bodies. But how will the head feel after five hundred years dead?

A NEW CONFIDENCE IN A PERFECT WORLD

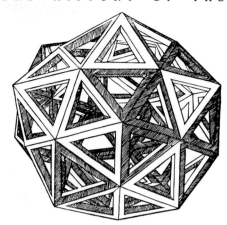

A NEW CONFIDENCE and a perfect world sounds very much like utopia. Many predictions of the future depict utopia, presumably because somehow we figure the future must turn out better than the present! Maybe we learn, maybe we don't.

During this century we are going to look at both sides of the coin with *Robopathic Labor* and *Androidism*, the arrival of new *Gurus and Masters*, a *Second Earth* and the extraordinary new technology that can tunnel the Earth, bring cryogenic suspension deaths back to life and jump through time. We will examine a *Bounded Universe, Gray Holes* and the science of the *Benevolent Circle*.

Before we get to these specifics we might take a look at this new confidence and the perfection it has engendered, for this may be the subtle under-body of galactic enterprise during this new century. The human race may find itself riding the crest of a high wave with a super-powerful force available in all life-forms but perhaps also, we may find this power only on the surface of life with still the same undiscovered depths of consciousness as much a mystery as ever.

If technology reaches a point, which it seems it might, where there are no longer any glitches to iron out; that machines in the broadest sense are doing everything for mankind; that leisure is available in dollop size chunks and the central heating doesn't break down — what would such a state of existence create in man himself?

It will almost be as though there is no entropy remaining — that everything in life that emits will be readmitted — all energy forms will be

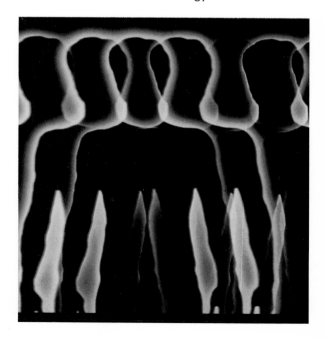

entrapped and reserved for further use. Everything will be clean, sharp, Swiss plus! How will this touch man's inner self?

For there are deeper levels within mankind which cannot ever be satisfied simply by the abandonment of drudgery. Dealing with the "synthetics" of life's process is one task which we may ultimately accomplish but then what?

The 20th century cannot be called an age of perfection, for we have not yet conquered or understood many of the "glitches" of life. We still suffer from horrendous diseases, terrible wars and appalling violence and yet there is already a strong spiritual seeking in existence which has arisen out of a deeper search inside the human psychology. This seeking comes from a greater degree of wealth and good fortune for it is invariably followed by those who have mastered the fundamentals of normal life and reached a point of self discovery which goes beyond mundanity. The 26th century might well be an enlarged version of today's spiritual search mode. Perhaps we shall then see what Gautama the Buddha called the turning of the "Wheel of Dharma" once more. For this would certainly entail some very strange and miraculous arrivals on Earth's surface.

GURUS AND MASTERS

TWO THOUSAND FIVE HUNDRED YEARS AGO Buddha achieved enlightenment, an indescribable and magnificent state far beyond all other states of being. During the same span of life, no less than eleven other men found enlightenment and existed on Earth in the Middle and Far East as teachers within a higher state of existence than has ever been seen perhaps until the 20th century.

Buddha foretold that the Wheel of Dharma turns once every 25 centuries and, counted on the modern calendar, that brings us to the end of the 20th century, to the very days that we are reading this book. He stated that the Wheel would need another "push" at around this time, for it is running down to such an extent that the presence of many spiritual leaders is needed to take us all through into another major period of our history. Whether we like it or not, the lives today of people such as J.Krishnamurti, Shree Rajneesh, U.G.Krishnamurti, Ramana Maharshi, Da Free John, Baba Ramdas and others, represent that new push towards change.

These men have created much fire and brimstone during the last few decades, with J.Krishnamurti being declared the new "World Teacher", Rajneesh bringing so many problems to the American nation with his gentle and sometimes frightening message of love and freedom and now the intellect and power of Da Free John and U.G.Krishnamurti's message

of doom and disaster. It is as though these men have attained enlightenment in order to shock us out of a sleep that we were not even aware was happening.

Alan Watts, the religious philosopher, stated during the early part of this century, that man is not awake when waking and asleep when dreaming. He is dreaming all the time and will one day wake up and find himself in heaven!

Perhaps this waking discovery of heaven will occur in the 25th century. The new message of meditation and love has become an international one with millions of people dropping out of everyday life in order to become disciples of one master or another. Many people find the whole change towards spiritual seeking confusing and troubling. Politicians do their best to stop people such as Rajneesh from ever landing in one country long enough to say anything, for the result of too much orange clothing or wooden beads would be a break down in the order that they believe is the right one.

Rajneesh continues to speak against politics, organized religion and most of the other established foundations of this society and strangely, when we look more closely at his words, rather than his Rolls Royces, we find that he has a lot in common with the findings of science. His message of "oneness" with life and "wholeness" tallies exactly with that of David Bohm, though seen from the Eastern eye rather

THE POWER OF THE SPIRIT

than Western science. It is almost as though such a man must shock us into turning our heads and listening. The shock may sometimes be a negative one but at least it makes us look.

This Wheel of Dharma, then, has begun its turn and the philosophers have said that it will gain full spin only after a few hundred years of pressure have elapsed. Perhaps, therefore we of the 20th century in our early appreciation or hatred of our living Masters, are the pioneers of this new move towards spiritual understanding. Perhaps the people of the 25th century will look back in their history books and examine us — talk our names and study what we began — a beginning that helped result in the perfection and confidence of their time.

It is difficult to make predictions of a spiritual future for it entails the necessity of bringing new masters and gurus to the scene and we can hardly do this convincingly. The very nature of the guru is one which demands individuality. All the Masters of this age are entirely different from one another. Indeed, one of their perspectives in teaching is that no two masters can be alike in any respect. Even if they do have the same message it will be tinged with alternative methods or attitudes which we will only recognize after the event.

But one thing that stands out in the new sciences and their alikeness to the new religions sprouting up in the West, is the development of scientific theories surrounding Bohm, Sheldrake and Prigogine and for this part of the book we will bring some interesting facts to the forefront in an hypothesis which may well be the grounding for what will be seen during the centuries to come.

Consider once again the concepts that Sheldrake has propounded — that everything in existence is made up of "form-fields" which help create the shapes and forms of everything. We have seen that the DNA cell does not appear to contain anything which dictates where it should go. That a brain cell has no obvious way of knowing that it should be a brain cell or a rock cell or a toe cell. What gives it the "knowledge" of where to settle in the shape of things to come?

So this proposal that there are morphogenetic fields everywhere around us, aiding life in all forms to become what it is, can be seen as a solution to the question. For those who doubt this concept Sheldrake uses, here again, the analogy of the TV set. If we were to look at a TV set without any knowledge of how it works we might first think that the pictures on the screen were created by little people inside the box.

Upon realizing that this was not so we might then investigate the tubes and electronic circuitry inside the box and assume that the interaction between them was the cause of the pictures. If we were then told, in our ignorance, that this was not so, but the picture emerged because of some outside signal coming to the box, we might say that this was impossible and doggedly experiment with the parts inside, in the determination that we will one day prove that there cannot be subtle waves coming from a transmission studio. This is the analogy that Sheldrake provides for doubting physicists and biologists — that the form fields he suggests exist, are like the transmission waves of the TV company and that the investigations into atomic and particle physics are being operated by scientists who look upon morphogenetic forms in the same way as the ignorant investigator who might look upon a TV.

Earth's Masters will define our spiritual future

If we accept the morphogenetic field concept, many fascinating developments can be deduced for the future. And they result, in the last analysis in a very revealing view of our resident Masters and gurus.

As a first step — take the form-field idea and apply it to particles. If form-fields influence the way that matter evolves into shape then perhaps it also influences the way in which all actions are happening in relation to those particles. When a scientist looks at a particle, the very act of looking creates a form-field. Every action that is undertaken creates a different field. Even if the scientist happens to

be wearing spectacles or a brown coat, or if he has had a fight with his wife or came to work in a bad traffic jam, each of these events will change his or her form-fields and therefore will also change the way that he comes to the experiment and thus the way he "sees" the particles. Taking it a step further we might even say that the scientist creates *with* the particles, the form that the particle takes. The scientist and the particle are making their own form-field — or — the scientist and the particle are making each other.

We can extend such a hypothesis still more and bring it into the realms of everyday life. Suppose that these form-fields also exist within our normal daily lives — at home, in our relationships, work, fears, all our acts while waking and sleeping. If we create the form fields which then in turn and continuously create us, we are constantly making our lives —

scientifically — what they are. Our harmonious or dis-harmonious activities in life are therefore all governed and created by such fields of form. Crime, fear, war and any of the other more negative live-forms could then be termed "Fear-fields".

The Masters of the East have being talking about "Buddhafields" for centuries — fields of energy that extend from enlightened beings and surround those who come into their presence. Perhaps these forms of existence will be identified by the 25th century and operate in a concrete and sensual fashion.

We may even see the form-fields of disease identified and thereby diverted. If we consider, for example, that the disease AIDS has its own morphological fields which are created and then enhanced by AIDS sufferers, perhaps there are far deeper truths buried under the normal medical view of illness.

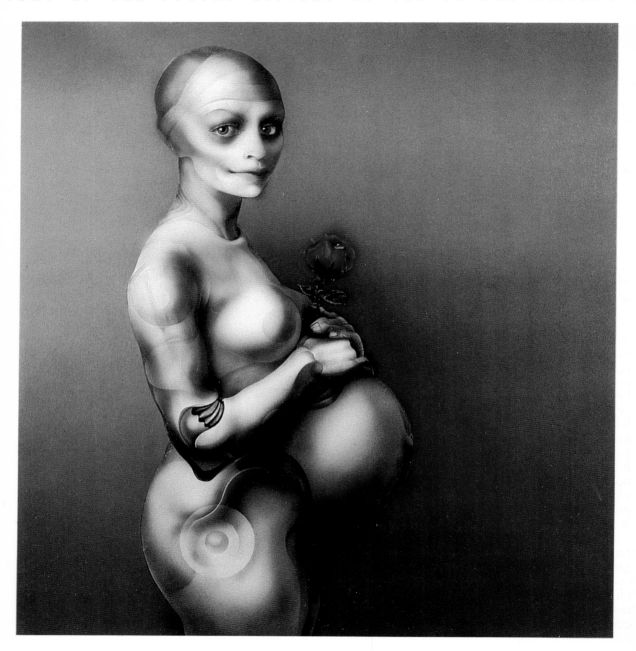

ANDROIDISM

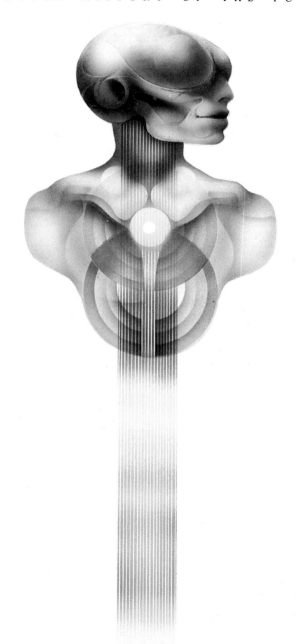

MAN HAS BEEN IMAGINING robots for a very long time. The motion picture "Metropolis", made earlier this century, proposed a world in which robotocism had already reached major advancement and pictured one of the most beautiful of "her" kind. Writers such as Isaac Asimov, Brian Aldiss, and Harry Harrison have depicted the robot or android in many forms and the movie world is peppered with all types, sizes and moods of robotic technology. The great cult movie *Blade Runner* brought us one of the most extravagant and imaginative forms of the human android — *The Replicant*.

Today, in the 20th century, real "live" robots are still only machines that operate other machines. They have not yet reached any advanced state and certainly do not much appear as human-like devices, walking on legs and using hands, powered from brains in heads. This is still too difficult for technology to achieve except perhaps in the most advanced labs. Beside anything else, getting a mechanical creature to walk like a human is the most difficult of the tasks facing technologists. It takes a million different nerve responses, balance techniques and gravity defiances — billions of brain responses and a host of other mechanical processes. Humans do it all day without a single thought.

Another of the many challenges facing roboticists is the creation of robotic sight. A group in Japan has recently devised a computer chip in which a layer of electronic photo-sensors takes the place of human rods and cones in the retina. Silicone layers contain computerized memory cells which can process visual signals and another chip performs similar processes to those of the vision centers of the brain. The device is considered capable of being used in robotic machines.

Still within the sensory patterns of human replication a human-like olfactory model is being built at the Robotics Institute of Carnegie Mellon University with tiny gas-sensitive semiconductors that can detect smells by reactive measures. Electrical impulses are sent by these semiconductors to a computer which can then identify the gas which caused the response.

Robotic hands are now highly advanced and can do many useful tasks such as breaking eggs and whipping the contents into a scrambled result for cooking!

What we are seeing then is the partial development of those bits of the human replicant that will eventually come together and make the complete robot. The move always, though, is to advance towards human-like machines which operate human activities in place of or beside humans. And this development, if taken into the future leads naturally to two different fields of enterprise: the mechanical robotic machine and then perhaps later, the android.

Computerized, semiconductor robots would seem to be not more than a step or two away — perhaps achieving prominence even during the next century so that much of the industrial need for mechanical aid might reach fulfillment in motor industries, computer industries and even office work, medical diagnosis or legal practice. Advanced robots could be seen in the home performing domestic tasks such as cooking, cleaning or security functions with limited human relating abilities operating voice responses such as answering the telephone and acting as "servants". But ultimately the mechanical robot will only ever achieve a limited human response ability for the human being is not built of semiconductors and computer relays. Only the biological replication of mankind can come close to

ROBOPATHICS

mankind himself and this is the era of the android.

By definition, the word "android" has its roots in the greek word "andros" meaning "of man" so that android means "looking like man." It would seem equally possible then, that with the ascendance of woman in our near future, we may also see "womandroids." There is, however, something of a dichotomy in the process which could be fulfilled by the arrival of human replication, for what constitutes something manlike as opposed to man-ly. If we

reach the stage of being able to give birth to human beings through "test-tube" science are the results of such births androids or humans? Does an android have a soul? When is a human human and when is an android not a human?

Stringing together a biological replicant in the same fashion as we construct a robot seems more in the realms of Frankinsteinian horror stories than likely scientific advance. It would seem, therefore, that any androidal configuration in the future would have to do with the building of creatures through mutational growth which might or might not be successful. The answer in the motion picture *Blade Runner* was the restriction of the lifespan and the creation of humanoids that had super-human powers such as greater strength and agility, but the final outcome in the person of the hero's lover, was a genuine human-android with a full set of human characteristics — a biologically devised human being.

The final stage of android science then would be the ability to make ourselves — which we do anyway!

SECOND
EARTH

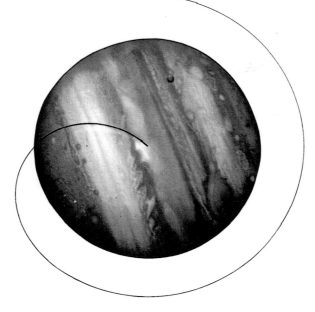

I T IS PROPOSED THAT BY THE 25th century mankind will be colonizing space effectively. He will have found alternative methods of living on other planets, on the moon and perhaps on Mars. It may be that he has found ways using economic drive systems such as the Scramjet which operates on the basis of converting hydrogen atoms through the heat generated (about 4,000 degrees F) by the speed of the jet into fuel to drive the jet still faster.

Such methods would be the beginning of travel to other habitable planets.

But ultimately the most difficult task is going to be that of the pioneers who have to conquer new terrain in adverse conditions, somewhat like the first pioneers of the American continent who had to deal with vast areas of mountain and land under all manner of unpredictable circumstances.

Such matters as the psychological state of the people "moving in" to the new planetary conditions would become highly important and the choice of those to begin such a fresh community would have to come from only a very small sector of humans and animals. It may be, in fact, more suitable to operate the early pioneering aspects by robot technicians. These would be sent in to complete the early parts of the work — building homes or working areas and setting up the ideal conditions for the second wave of occupancy — the humans.

Once the first structures were in existence and operating under habitable conditions, the next likely visitors, according to NASA-related sources will be tourists! Wealthy visitors to any space colonized center would have to pay in the range of $1,000,000 by today's financial standards, to take a space craft to the Moon or Mars and spend a few days touring the massive glass structures that would be built from Moon resources. Glass can be extracted from the rock and makes a better building material than aluminum which tends to warp with temperature differences.

After the tourists would come the commuters!

Once the colonization had been achieved, workers would be needed to operate the new world and these might have the option to return to Earth on regular visits rather than initially bring their families with them.

An inter-planetary "bus" would move from planet to planet picking up commuting passengers and returning them to their home base within months or eventually weeks. The link up would be done via space stations, to which the commuter would take a shuttle and enter a module which would be launched to the bus and interlock there.

Aboard the bus would be natural vegetable gardens for fresh food and large enough living areas to enjoy a relatively comfortable journey. Upon arrival at the final destination the original module would be launched once more for landing and the bus would continue to its next destination without needing to land at all.

Of course, this would be the transport for the masses — i.e. those who cannot afford their own private space craft or the price of chartering it. There will be others in the future who may travel in the lap of luxury aboard the future equivalent of Concorde or the Lear Jet.

Even today there are drawing-board plans to convert ordinary airliners into orbital space vehicles. Those responsible, in Atlanta, Georgia propose conversions of anything from a DC-9 to Concorde, by altering the wing structures from the conventional swept formation to perpendicular. Rocket engines would power the crafts and after being towed into orbit they would "skate" to their destination.

Craft in the future, therefore, might be created that would operate both on Earth and in space, allowing owners or passengers to travel literally from their homes directly to Mars!

While on board your private space vehicle you would of course enjoy a variety of entertainments, including the "Video Helmet's" provision for holographic cinema created by moving holographic shows of your choosing. Video Helmets are already in existence today,

devised by the Aerospace Human Factors Division of NASA's Ames Research Center who have created a working prototype which is presently designed so that the wearer can control displays within the helmet by the movement of the head. The helmet does not, of course, yet provide holographic video, but still a three-dimensional screen, which results in a sense, for the wearer, of being inside the display within the helmet. Such a three-dimensional aspect, although not holographic, makes for involvement. The helmet is presently used for command

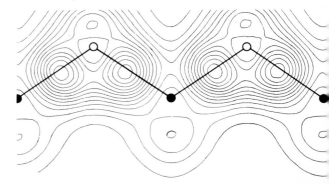

and even the emotions of the user could not be computerized into "Fashion-Feature" movies and adventures in which we would be able to go to Africa, Mars, or any imagined location and live out the actual experience, without even leaving our arm-chairs. The arm-chairs, of course, would be constructed from form-fields that don't in fact result in anything solid, but when we sit down, they take up the morphogenetic field of the concept "arm-chair". The practical joke of removing chairs from behind people about to sit down might no longer be operable!

Looking still further into space, beyond our own galaxy, we will not perhaps be able to travel such distances by normal means. If by the 25th century we are colonizing the far-flung galaxies, the traveling will need to be done by the freezing of human beings in a nitrogen solution — a kind of cryogenic suspension. Just to give some idea of the distances involved, if we consider the distance from Earth to the Sun — 93 million miles — to be one inch, then the nearest star — Alpha Centauri — would be four and a third miles from the sun! In terms of time, any space vehicle would take almost two decades just to leave this galaxy (depending on orbital changes in the planets) given our present maximum speed of space travel.

Even using fusion rockets, if they are ever developed, it would still take over half a century to travel to another star. Unless... we consider the possibility of *Time Jumping*.

purposes — to operate robots in manufacturing and working conditions, using LCD display systems with a tiny TV.

The Video Helmet is an obvious device for entertainment in the future and given the final holographic technology, it would be a life-like experience for the wearer.

As a further development of such a helmet, the future may see more advanced systems that permit the user to enter into a scenario and actually create its story. Given sensory connections through bio-chip technology there is no reason why the thoughts and imaginings

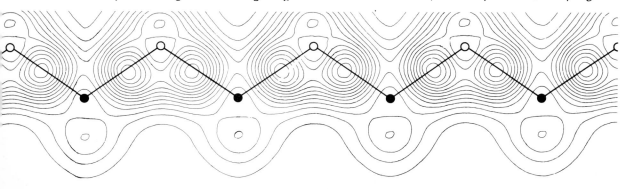

TIME

We HAVE LOOKED ALREADY at time travel and time folding — at the ideas of the implicate order of the universe — the metaphor of holographic time and space. But what about the enigma facing physicists at the moment, in which particles seem to move from one place to another without ever passing the space in between. Where would such a notion take us in terms of our own ability to move from here to there?

Like many things in physics during the 20th century, it all began with an assumption based on the discoveries and thoughts of Albert Einstein.

Einstein proposed that if a pair of particles flew apart, an observer looking at one of them and thereby affecting it, would not immediately affect the other. How, after all, could one particle "know" what the other was doing? But in fact, according to tests based on calculations done by a British physicist, J.S.Bell, that is exactly what happens. A Frenchman named Alain Aspect split correlated pairs of photons and then fired them in opposite directions, shifting a polarizing filter in front of one of the detectors while both photons were in flight. The first photon was shown to "know" the effect on the other. The experiment is somewhat like the stories of closely related people such as twins, knowing what is happening to one another even though separated by large distances.

Such a result steps over the boundaries of reasonable science and enters the realms of the fairy tale — or what some might call a "Looking Glass Universe." The only clear extrapolation from such an experimental conclusion is that there is no *here* and *there* but that *here* is the same as *there*. The physicists call this conclusion *the nonlocality* of space and time.

The first response to such an unreasonable circumstance is that such nonlocality applies only at the microcosmic level and not at the *macro*cosmic. In other words, sub-atomic particles such as photons might be able to jump through time, or be in two places at the same time, but we macro-humans cannot.

But macro-humans are made of sub-atomic particles such as photons. In fact our whole existence is made of them right down to the hydrogen atoms that fill space and matter. So how come they can do it and we can't?

If we add to this existential weirdness the hypothesis that our view of the universe is governed by our conditioned awareness of it — in other words that we see the way things are only because we have learned to see them that way — then perhaps there are other ways that we *could* see things that encompass the nonlocality of existence.

If we think back to the concepts which outline the enfolded universe as one holographic-type organism from which our *unfoldment* creates the shapes and perceptions we are happy with, then it may be that we simply *unfold* the way that we do because we always did.

Take a simple example. If we take a narrow, flat sheet of paper with two sides and if we take each end of the narrow strip and we twist them so that the two ends can be joined with a piece of scotch tape we see that there are no longer two flat surfaces but one continuous roundelay of one surface. This is called the "moebius strip" and illustrates the way we can perceive reality in two different ways using one item.

Our present understanding of universal truths is based on our conditioned response to our surroundings. We think therefore we are — but actually it is also true the other way — we are, therefore we think and it may even be so that we are not even though we think! For thought may not be ours but something created by the cosmos.

Our linear approach to life — cause and therefore effect — is subject to a total about face. It may be that effect comes first and then we face a continuous cause.

Take time — if what Bohm says is correct — all time, past, present and future occupy one place — now, the present. All the past events that have ever been have accumulated into the very moment that you are looking at this WORD. The future is also contained within the moment that you contemplate the NEXT word.

And if the particles of which we are all made can move from one spot to another without traveling between the two, perhaps they also exist, as matter, in past, present and future at the same time.

JUMPING

With such a barrage of hypotheses we move into a future containing such devices as would be common only aboard the U.S.S. Enterprise or in the movie Dune. Travel by teleportation, space travel by enfoldment, transmogriphication of human shapes, body repair by biological re-growth of human parts, no natural death — simply a change of body and an ability to reach any part of the universe instantly.

Airports would disappear along with cars and other solid transport forms. No roads, no traffic jams, no accidents (except perhaps inside the teleportation chambers!), no need for fuels, so no pollution. Too good to be true.

But such a future would be the direct result of the time-jumping ability of nonlocality.

HAVING LOOKED BRIEFLY at the possibility of instant travel, we now come back down to Earth — literally — to look at a totally different but still very fast method of getting from A to B.

This time we are not traveling through space but through matter at close to the center of the planet.

Man has long been eager to dig holes in his planet and travel down them. The era of the Industrial Revolution in Europe and the United States saw the beginning of massive

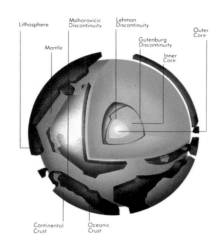

Victoria Station — thousands of miles in length! The tunnel would be built to contain tracks which would stabilize a vehicle using magnetic equalizers — the train suspended in the center of a vacuum and capable of speeds of ten miles per second — taking around 52 minutes to complete the journey.

The magnetic system works on the basis of superconductor magnets which weigh very little and alternate the poles of direct current, literally throwing the train forward through the tunnel.

The trains would operate on

MIDDLE EARTH

tunneling through mountain terrain. One of the longest tunnels was built in Switzerland — 22 kilometers in length, but since then there has been nothing longer, though shortly we will be seeing the new Channel Tunnel which will extend from England under the sea to France.

But such efforts are not much more than a child digging in the sand of the beach if compared with plans that could be fulfilled during the middle of the next millennium.

Already theoretically possible, a tunnel might exist from New York's Grand Central Station to Bombay's

what is already known as "maglev"or magnetic levitation.

One of the biggest problems associated with a train which moves at such massive speeds is the gravitational force that would be exerted on the passengers. It's one thing for a US Airforce pilot to have his face flattened like a piece of raw meat, but few normal travelers would elect to undergo such pressures on a commuting journey to work in India each day.

The answer will lie in the operation of gravity as a field of force which can be controlled and decreased to an acceptable level. Passengers will not be aware that they are moving at all.

CRYOGENICS

Frozen Time

AND WHEN ALL THE TRAVELING is done and we reach the end of the journey, the last step will not be death — but suspension until the next life.

At least in theory — for there are some very interesting possibilities which the science of cryogenics may not yet have encountered. There are already many people, such as Charlie Chaplin, for example, settled comfortably inside cylinders filled with liquid nitrogen, in states of cryogenic suspension. The hope, presumably, is that the body can be returned to life when science and medicine have conquered all sickness and come up with methods of bringing the dead back to life.

Liquid nitrogen, maintained at 196 degrees below zero looks like crystal clear water and rests amidst clouds of vapor in large vaults such as the one in the ALCOR Life Extension Foundation of Fullerton, California where the cryogenic suspension system does not trouble to store the whole body of the hopeful dead, but only the head!

The idea is that some time away, perhaps in the 25th century, it will be possible to work on the cells of each head to restore life to them and then clone a new body from a single cell and attach it to the revived head.

Cryogenic suspension has been around since the 1960s when Robert Ettinger from Highland Park Community College published a book entitled *The Prospect of Immortality*. The idea gave life to cryogenic societies around the

world, all of which have the same philosophy — that dying is only another potentially curable sickness. The cost of suspension is up to $100,000 for the whole body and just $30,000 for the head alone. Though it is not clear how long this will maintain the necessary supervision should cures for the dead take a little longer than anticipated! In any event, at the end of the 20th century the whole subject of cryonics is not taken so very seriously amongst scientists who specialize in biological freezing techniques. The body freezer ideologists are regarded somewhat as fringe technicians with a misguided view of the processes and their potential. The main problem is in the considerable damage that is done to the tissue during the freezing process itself. It seems that cryogenic freezing may actually be the reason why the bodies in question could never be revived. A sort of Catch 22 situation.

What we may well see by the middle of the next millennium is the existence of body-part warehouses in which various or all parts of the body are kept frozen for surgical use in living but damaged bodies. This process is more likely to be successful because each form of tissue in the body can need a special kind of controlled situation in freezing techniques in order to be usable again later.

But the concept of revivifying whole bodies or heads to be added to "new" bodies forms another more esoteric problem for it connects with the present day understanding that consciousness resides in a body or head while in a frozen state. Upon the death of a human being the cellular structure — i.e. that part of us which is purely physical, may remain intact and there might come a time when this shell can be brought back to life through chemical or electrical means. But how do we propose to reinject the whole complexity of consciousness into a dead body?

If Sheldrake's and Bohm's beliefs prove to be accurate, there is much more to life than the body. There is a constantly flowing energy form around and within the body which has developed from the whole past of mankind and also from the life in question.

The re-birth of a dead and long-gone body would create something that might in effect be a sudden and unnatural grafting of human nature into completely new form-fields, without consciousness and without any connection what ever with the intervening time span. The new human would in effect be without emotions, without those things that are learned and absorbed through a normal healthy life, resulting in a creature which would be disastrously disoriented and perhaps devoid of the presence of existence. But these things do not enter our heads right now and certainly they don't enter the frozen heads in the suspended nitrogen caskets. But these will be the problems facing any cryogenic science of the future. It may even affect the frozen organs that are taken from one body and implanted in another.

In fact the whole aura of morphogenetic fields might prove to be of interest to medicine in its dilemma surrounding organ implant. It seems that the rules proposed by Sheldrake that imply the difficulty of forming a morphogenetic field for the first time, might apply here. If we remember, to create a new crystallized structure is always difficult the first time but becomes progressively easier as the experiment is repeated until the formation seems to happen very quickly and without effort after many repetitions.

If we look at body-part implants we see that the very early attempts made by, for example, heart surgeons, to replace ailing hearts with fresh ones from elsewhere, were largely thwarted by an unwillingness of the host body to accept the new organ. As these operations continue they achieve greater success and this may not be because the host body has problems not accepting the organ itself, but the form-fields that accompany it. These are, after all still the "alien" form-fields of the previous owner perhaps still intact around the organ. Quite a bit of adjustment could be needed for the personal form-field to integrate with the new/old field and additionally the entire existential form-fields involved in the whole area of organ transplant might need considerable adjustment before we can take advantage of the change physically.

Put in another way, it may be that the problems with body-part transplants occur because the form-fields around the parts being brought together simply don't work in harmony at the outset. A foreign part, after all, will have its own set of fields which derive from the body from which it has been taken and when brought in contact with a new set of fields there might initially be some "argument" between them which could result in a rejection of the new part. The only way to resolve such a situation will be, of course, to be entirely familiar with form-field technology.

We NOW APPROACH THE END of the half millennium.

And it is almost as though we are already in a kind of fairy tale world, with invisible fields of energy, forms of consciousness that cannot today be easily fathomed. With time travel and strange sciences that may create a planetary existence far beyond anything we could imagine now.

But the overall picture that emerges is one of opposites. It is almost as though many of the

GRAY HOLES

Faster than light particles that defy Einstein's Laws

BENEVOLENT CIRCLE

Transforming the vicious-circles

old ideas about life have come once again to the forefront. We are no longer thinking in terms of particles and solid matter, of moving through life in a forward motion, but more in terms of flowing fields of energy that take us into magical lands of unreason and apparent chaos.

We can see this most readily in universal states of understanding. Scientists used to figure in terms of an everlasting, infinite universe that went on through space and time to some vast distance, whereas now they think in terms of space and time being everywhere always. That the whole of our imagined universe is actually at our finger tips, everywhere we look. In this way of perceiving life it is as though we are in the presence of a bounded universe which we can literally touch by reaching out our hands.

If time is not fixed in a linear mode then we can access it any time we like, past, present and future. If space is holographic and not linear then we have all of it right here inside our own cells.

Such ideas give a new vision and one that may be hard for us to swallow.

One of the other most recent hypotheses arises out of the suspicion that our belief in the constant speed of light may be unfounded. All of Einstein's scientific paradigms were based on the supportable certainty that light *always* travels at 186,000 miles per second. But with photons that jump from one place to another and often also disappear, it is even being considered that perhaps there are forces which can move at 187,000 miles per second. This would, therefore, in effect give us an entity which could move constantly backwards in time.

Black Holes, then, might become Gray Holes for if their force is great enough to "suck" light into their center, why not other particles which move faster still. Perhaps on the other side of the consuming black hole there really is another universe which mirrors this one in reverse — a sort of anti-matter, anti-time opposite constantly traveling backwards!

And of course, given a bounded and

BENEVOLENT CIRCLE
Transforming the vicious-circles

available universe with all forms of time available to us, we would inevitably arrive at the conclusion that there are no rules, no certainties and all forms of life or non-life are possible.

With such an understanding, concepts of morality and rules of play will vanish for all time. It becomes wildly impossible under such conditions to come near to accurate prediction for we are not even dealing with the standard variables we have in our lives today. Everything is essentially blown to pieces. All we can hope is that such awesome powers represent a benevolent existence that brings us back to our source. But the problem with this is that our source may not be at all what we imagine it to be.

The more obscure Eastern traditions state that life began in a void and that this void was a beginningless nothingness which lacked any kind of formation, even lacking the idea of a lack of formation. It was absolute nothingness without reason, form or being. At some unspeakable and non-temporal moment the void developed a ripple or a wave which instantly resulted in some form of existence. The theory is that if a void is able to cause something such as a wave then it is no longer a void! The wave that arose was in the form of an awareness of itself — in other words the wave was a kind of mirror of itself — a second-void. But in so doing the void became a personality — the mirror of itself was a mask or a fake of its original nothingness. Then this replicant of the void arose, looked at itself and decided to become mankind. Mankind thereafter looked upon himself, now outside the void and saw that he was man. But this vision was not real — it was a reflection and therefore never actually existed except as a reflection. Man's whole effort since that beginning has been to find his way back to the original void and the only way he can do it is to cease being anything reflected and become nothingness once more. This then is the spirtual quest and perhaps the way of the benevolent circle — what a way to go!

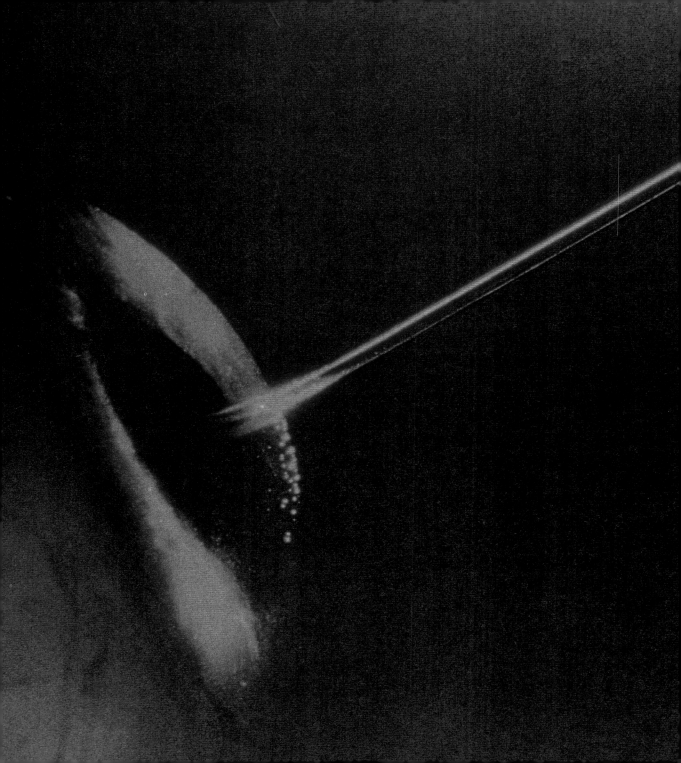

C6

C E N T U R Y

2500-2600

THE
RING
OF
ROSES

"Ring a ring of roses,
pocket full of posies,
atishoo, atishoo,
we all fall down."

Song of the plague
—Middle Ages.

	THEO-SCIENCE	BODY-COLOGY	PHILO-THINKING	ASTRO-NOMICS	MAN-SCIENCE
2500 • 2510	**RETURN TO THE VOID** Coming full circle to man's beginning.				
2510 • 2520		**HEAD-GAMES** Sports in the mind.			**COMPUTER LAW** Birth of AICS - Acquired Integrated Circuit Syndrome.
2520 • 2530			**TECHNO-SCIENTOLOGY** The old man Hubbard reborn.		
2530 • 2540				**GALACTIC WAR** The beginnings of conflict again, on a larger scale.	
2540 • 2550					
2550 • 2560				**WHO'S FRIENDLY?** Out there in space there will be some strange events.	**HUMAN POTENTIAL** Sport brings hope to man's freedom.
2560 • 2570	**THE NEW PRIESTHOOD** The church is dead, science transformed.				**EVERYTHING NOT FORBIDDEN** A new science of what not to do.
2570 • 2580					
2580 • 2590	**GOD'S GROWING** The confidence has brought head-strength.				**THE MEGA PENTATHLON** Extraordinary feats of energy.
2590 • 2600			**HEAD-STRENGTH** The mind revolution will not affect all.		**THE LEISURE LIFE** Too much time off gives problems.

Age of Confidence

2500 • RETURN TO THE VOID

It is said that mankind once was nothing — a void without waves of motion Then a wave occured and mankind was born a mirror — one day perhaps we will return to the void

2540 • THE BIRTH OF AICS

Acquired Integrated Circuit Syndrome is the computer equivalent of AIDS — a disease amongst chips! It may sound like a joke but read on, it's deadly serious

2570 • MEGA-SPORTS

Pentathlons in the future will be thousands of miles long, with super-human strength required by the contestants — all in the course of competition

THE LEISURE LIFE
AND COMPUTER LAW

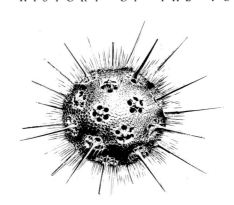

WE HAVE ALREADY LOOKED AT the concept that mankind creates his own diseases — styling them closely with the mood of each age — almost as though they reflect the condition he is in. AIDS and cancer could be seen as reflections of the 20th century, mirroring the complexity, the anxiety and the sexual repression of the late 1900s in the same way as the Black Death or the Great Plague mirrored the poor physical conditions of the Middle Ages. And we can extend this concept through to the second half of the next millennium, beginning our search for reasons and the likely form of dis-ease at the beginning of this new century — the 26th. For this century will be of great significance, bringing as it will, the bizarre results of confidence and leisure — of computers that do everything and people who face a new kind of freedom which may not be so free after all.

The 26th century is seen as a dark time — almost the equivalent of the 5th and 6th centuries in Europe known as The Dark Ages, with Galactic Wars looming, strong new religions and dramatic changes in all forms of human life. We will examine first the results of *The Leisure Life* and *Computer Law*, which unexpectedly perhaps, contain the elements of human and bio-technological sickness.

In order to understand the processes that will lead us to greater leisure, we must first take a look at how global economy works on a grand scale. We can most simply examine this by imagining a sort of graph or table in which the product of a country or countries is at one end of the table — agriculture, technology, lumber, glue, cement, fuel etc. — and what these basic "building blocks" go into — food, computers, furniture, homes, cars etc. This forms then a

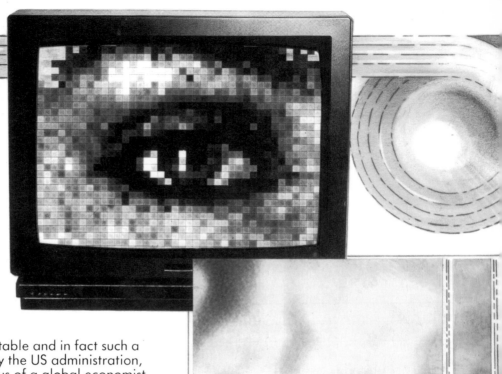

kind of input-output table and in fact such a device is operated by the US administration, based upon the genius of a global economist named Wassily Leontief originally from the Soviet Union.

We have also taken advice for this aspect of the book from Dr. Andreas Landert, one of the world's most renowned Swiss economists who, amongst other things provides many of the economy graphs for *The Wall Street Journal*.

The result of operating such an input-output table provides a picture of how the ultimate consumer will respond to conditions such as war, overpopulation, technological or scientific change. And in this way we can see clearly the future environment our descendants will face. The main feature of the system is that it is directly related to the real world — using practical statistics and facts to come to social conclusions, rather than relying on theory which may not have any grounding.

In our input-output chart of the 26th century

we would expect to see, at the input end, a highly efficient provision of available materials, mostly operated by robotic labor and technological farming, remembering, at the same time, our indications of the relevance of morphic fields — those form-fields which coordinate the habits of creation. If everything is operated by mechanistic and bio-chip technology then this will bring the appropriate form-fields to the eventual product consumed by society. As a simple analogy we might "taste" the difference between heavily chemically impregnated milk, known today as *UHT* milk and natural unpasturized milk. Those of us who have drunk milk directly after the cow has given it, will know the difference! Given a highly mechanized and robotic labor force for the input end of our table, we might consider the likely implications on the social structure at the other end.

An additional feature to weave into our prediction, recently experienced in a big way in computer oriented organizations in the States, is the *Computer Virus*!

A bunch of young computer programming geniuses in Pakistan decided in 1984 to create a program that would prevent disc copying of copyrighted programs. Their "glitch" design was such that it was extremely difficult to detect and could be placed within any programmed disc that needed protection against pirating. However, the result was somewhat different. The particular instruction embedded within the protection program was designed to "jump" into the pirated disc, into any hard disc and even down modem lines to other computers. Once it reaches the victim system it instantly wipes clean all data on the system! Computer operators were given some

nasty shocks on arriving in their offices in the morning, to find their total computer memory bank — blank! In the United States, at time of writing, special screening systems have been set up to look over programs before they are used or copied — a kind of inoculation system against the computer virus which we might call *Acquired Integrated Circuit Syndrome* or *AICS*. And as we watch computer technology transform into bio-computer technology, the implications for *AICS* are endless — infestation of global computer networks with dis-ease on the scale of any human sickness or greater. For as computers are able to digest and suggest information at a far greater speed and efficiency than humans, so also presumably they will operate in the same way with disease.

So — to sum up our somewhat complex thesis in this early part of the 26th century — we have:

1. Mechanized input allied with appropriate form-fields
2. Greater leisure, perhaps leading to a kind of boredom syndrome and
3. *AICS.*   There will be those who can already see the inter-connections between these items of possibility, but for those who don't we propose the following conclusion. Given the form-fields inherent in an artificial intelligence system which provides the basic fuel of life — food, materials and power, together with a slowing down of adrenalin within a leisure oriented social environment, linked with bio-chip viruses moving at the speed of light, mankind by the 26th century (or well before) could find himself contracting *AICS* directly from his home bio-computer network link-up and dying rather rapidly from a clean-wiped environmental cosmic memory.

If the memory system suggested earlier in this book, operates within the morphogenetic form-fields around us, presumably it can be potentially infected by the "glitches" of the bio-chip and we may find ourselves in the presence of existential or cosmic amnesia.

This would truly be silence on a grand scale!.

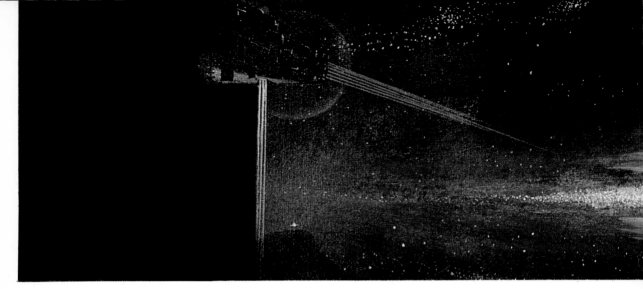

ALONGSIDE THIS RATHER AWE-INSPIRING return to the void, during a century which can be seen as perhaps the most disastrous in the history of mankind, we may also see galactic war.

When we have managed to approach the goals and certainties that we so eagerly seek today, when we have found the ultimate scientific balance and the permanent vacation, with some form of global harmony — i.e. we are not any more fighting each other — there will come the challenge of alien races and the possibility of striving through galactic dominance.

With a massive dose of some form of human virus, perhaps taking the shape suggested in the previous pages, Earth will be weakened and vulnerable to attack from any form of warring outside power. Perhaps there are species out there simply waiting for us to climb to the appropriate levels of advancement before striking down upon us and taking the advantages we have created in the future.

Many of the UFO enthusiasts and "observers" of the 20th century would certainly go along with such a concept, though whether the potential visiting aliens are benevolent or malicious will presumably depend on the state of the rest of the universe and the history that is

RETURN TO THE VOID — GALACTIC WAR

*Even 2000 light years away
the implications are devastating*

running concurrent to ours, out there.

For at least the last hundred years and in less identifiable forms, long before that, man has taken two views of the UFO phenomenon. Either he regards it with complete distrust and casts it off as nonsense or he believes that there are *extraterrestrials* visiting this planet all the time. There are so many very convincing accounts from so many different people that it is hard to state unequivocally that there is nothing happening — no smoke without *some* fire. Conversely astronomers have failed in all cases to successfully track a UFO sighting of any kind — there is no hard evidence whatever — at least not readily available.

The whole subject of whether they are there or not has become something of a cliche and perhaps some new approach is needed, for there is still much interest in the idea of UFOs. We might, for example, look at the question through the eyes of form-fields and say that if many people imagine, believe, expect that UFOs are there, then they must be in some form. We could say the same for ghosts or other para-psychological aspects of the supernatural. Ghosts may well be the results of remaining forms that have derived a habit from the physiological presence of living people — but after the death of that particular individual the form-field simply did not give up the visual aspect and so walks the nights clanking chains and groaning at not being able to disperse successfully.

Equally the "habit" of UFOs has become so well established within mankind's perceptive values that perhaps we have created them simply by creating them and the more we hear of others observing their presence, the more they will appear.

Much of the theorizing that surrounds alien presence suggests that because the sightings include inexplicable phenomena, such as fore-shortened light beams (i.e. beams of light which end after say 20 feet) then the aliens in question must be more advanced and therefore more intelligent than we are. This does not, of course, follow. The fact that a race of beings might develop in certain areas to a different extent to humans does not mean that they are generally more advanced — they may be terrific at fore-shortening light beams and hopeless at boiling eggs! And this gives rise to the other most prevalent human condition — the expectation that everything else outside the human race is either better or worse than the human race. It goes back once again to the old dualist approach combined with that very natural egotistic attitude to life which encompasses inferiority and superiority, both of which, as life potential aspects, it is suggested,

are meaningless.

The day that we reach a state of physiological contact with other species of life will be the day that we realize that nothing is better or worse than us but only different. It is this realization which can totally alter our perception of what may be in the rest of the universe. For, if the universe unfolds from a standard absolute into human nature, it may also unfold from the same absolute into anything it likes, in just the same way as oxygen and hydrogen can form either water (H_2O) or hydrogen peroxide (H_2O_2).

Given the increasingly unattractive state of planet Earth during the 26th century, with terrible diseases, no remaining Earth-bound challenges and perhaps a return to the Dark Ages, man may find himself happier off-board, traveling around the local galaxies using photon-drive or scramjet flight systems to move enormous distances into space with the ease of the 20th century jet liner or private craft. In such variance of activity another present-day aspect of life will alter.

Something that we rarely take into account in our view of the local universe, is the disproportionate view we have of our planet. Because we live as tiny creatures on what seems a giant world, we imagine that we are hugely visible to the rest of the galaxy. But if you, the reader, look out into that starry night, which star would you pick out as particularly significant and which planet? First of all, the nearest star is too far away to even reach in a life-time and the planets are invisible to the human eye. Even with a giant telescope there are so many planets in the heavens that the choice of one in particular as being likely to carry life is impossible. Why should we imagine that anyone a hundred thousand light years away should pay us any attention at all?

The situation will, however, alter radically once we are chuntering around in space as regularly as the down-town bus. There will be far more space-human presence and thus far

The New Priesthood

more likelihood of contact. UFOs may or may not visit us, but the day that we become UFOs ourselves will be the beginning of the future potential for galactic war.

And back on Earth, with the presence of a cosmic silence created by our new disease *AICS* and war in space raging on all fronts we will need to have some grounding to keep us from falling off the edge of the world. And the new priesthood that would more than likely result from such conditions would be strong and down-to-earth — perhaps even bio-technological.

We will need doctors who can cure the science we have created but the science will *be* the doctor, for bio-chip computer technology will have found its way not only into production and industry but also medicine, law, government and the human sciences. Who then, will cure the doctor? Only the medicine man will be left — witchcraft, superstition and black magic may live again in the form of the new priesthood.

HUMAN
POTENTIAL
SPORTS

IT IS NOTICEABLE IN TIMES of history when the world is in conflict, that sport becomes an increasing fascination. The 20th century has been witness to an even greater growth of spectator sport than ever before with almost manic fascination for football, baseball and athletic sports. The element of competition and the financial rewards have now brought sports activities to a pinnacle of passion. How will we see this escalate or deflate in the next centuries.

With the coming of space travel and lunar homes we may see some interesting new sports. How about Lunar Hurdling, for example? With a much lower gravity pull — approximately one sixth of that on Earth — the problem will not be getting over the hurdles, but getting back down to the ground again! Jumpers will be more like ski-jumpers with heights of up to 100 meters possible without much effort. Running at speed will be very difficult under such conditions for the sprinter will have to move with the torso and head almost level with the ground in order to avoid having the legs flip out from under.

Games of competitive sport will probably also include a spatial form of Le Mans — only this time it will not be in racing cars but super-fast space launches that will race from Earth to the moon, around the back of it and back to Earth again, a bit like large sailing yachts in space. The winners will be those who can make the best trajectory, stay the closest to the lunar surface and get back into Earth's atmosphere at the highest speed without burning up in the atmosphere. Space racing might also extend to a kind of space slalom, the vehicles darting in and out of strategically placed satellites which might have the tendency to move unpredictably.

Back on Earth sports will grow faster and

faster and will entail greater and greater skills. As touched on by Rupert Sheldrake in his piece in this book entitled *The Principles of Universal Habit*, morphogenetic fields will always increase the habitual learning skills of the sportsperson. This explains why in sprinting, for example, times recorded for the 100 meter dash always grow shorter. One wonders how far this can go! Some thirty years ago a runner named Bannister broke the "four-minute-mile," but today, almost any self-respecting Olympic runner can do the mile in well under this time. Athletes are so fast today that it seems every record is being broken the moment it is made — even without steroids!

Will we then see these distances run in two minutes by the 26th century? Or is there a threshold beyond which no human can go without physiological changes? Given Sheldrake's theories, if the distance can be covered by anything that moves, there is no reason why the body shouldn't be the machine to do it. We may see runners making the mile in under a minute, literally passing the spectator at a rate which will be difficult to see. A blur of light and sound will streak around the course leaving burning feet marks in the dust and taking several minutes to slow after the tape is broken.

In the realm of shot-put, discus or javelin, the muscular power of the body may grow potentially great enough to hurl various items enormous distances, despite gravitational forces. Stadiums will therefore need to be much larger or special force fields will be designed to stretch out beyond the javelin or shot in order to prevent accidents in the stands.

Group sports such as football or baseball could take on new proportions as the players

become faster and stronger, with pitches growing larger and goal posts narrower. The armor needed to protect the players will take the form of artificially created form-fields surrounding the body and causing the rapidly transiting ball to bounce back without harm.

In this way the players will be left freer to move without the encumbrances of padding.

The only national sport which may not substantially change is cricket which depends largely for its pleasure on the slowness and calm of the players, despite the ever increasing speed of the bowler's arm. The rest of the game requires a certain meditative spirit for its success. Hopefully this may remain the same even through to the 26th century.

But such sporting activities are all totally based in the thinking of the 20th century and over the next five hundred years the tone of sport is likely to alter far beyond our own limited participation in competition. But like everything in life, it could go one of several ways and we shall look at a few of the alternatives in these pages.

The Mega-Pentathlon

WITH THE RISE IN HUMAN physical power, endurance and speed would likely come an ever increasing desire to compete on higher and higher levels. Sport, if taken down to its roots, brings, more than any other human occupation, the hunting instinct and therefore direct connection with death — the risk of death. Even today, the human biological machines that perform the herculean tasks of Olympic challenge, have created in their appearance that of the mighty God who challenges life to the death. Simply watching runners and other athletes on our televisions or in the stadiums of sport produces a sense of unreality — the shining and glistening muscle

stretching and filled with tension almost to breaking point, suggests a toughening of human endurance which is reflected even in our fantasies in movies such as *Rocky* where power has reached an almost ridiculous level.

Muscle builders — "iron-pumpers" have almost created a new breed of humanity which would never even have been seen in the old *Charles Atlas* ads., in which this very first of muscle men pulled locomotives with chains. Never before the 20th century has there been such iron physical strength and should this develop still further over the next centuries it will be hard to find outlets sufficiently dangerous and demanding to satisfy them.

Mega-Pentathlons might entail year long races that are run on army-assault-course lines in which the competitors undertake unbelievable feats of competitive activity. We will likely see sports that are watched by the whole planetary system on holo-satellite TV in full four dimensional color right there in the living room as groups of challengers race across deserts and through Amazonian forests, encountering impossible tasks that bring them constantly close to death.

The runners will be capable of long periods of time under water without air provision and across the Sahara Desert without water, crossing the Alps with only the thin clothes on their backs and up and over Mount Everest without so much as a breathing tank or warm clothes.

Their food provision will be minimal, economically balanced to provide maximum protein and vitamins and a water supply that will be carried in tiny hydrogen-converting modules inside the mouth. The bodies of these competitors will have been conditioned since birth to the task of the Mega-Pentathlon, and huge financial reward will encourage them to take dreadful risks while the whole leisured world watches.

Above the competitors in the skies around them will be hovering craft filled with front-row seat spectators who will pay large sums to be present as the sports-people break their backs to win. Tennis, baseball, athletics and other modern-day sports will have nothing on the Mega-Pentathloners for speed, power and danger and almost in the same vein as the Roman Games, such sports will achieve ever increasing insanity in their desire to beat the last records. This will be sport gone crazy.

Head Games

OR WE COULD see entirely the opposite where the body-physical has lost its appeal through the out-doing of constant competitive attempts. Where the mind and the spirit combine instead of the body and the spirit. In this case, games such as bio-chip super-brain games will be played, in which the competitors remain safely seated in their homes, while operating through the same holo-satellite systems to fight against one another on a more intellectual level. They will create their own computer games, similar perhaps to the 20th century *Dungeons and Dragons*, in which the players make up the rules of the game as they go along and reproduce their wildest fantasies, including themselves in the adventure in the form of constructed story-lines — dangerous missions, spiritual or physical quests that range across the whole galaxy.

There would surely be no shortage of imagination with the most advanced technology available to formulate our dreams.

Then again, perhaps with the coming of a plethora of leisure and freedom, without the substance of spirit — as might be the case in a world close to another Dark Age — perhaps sport will vanish altogether and all we will have is holographic museums of the great sportsmen of the 20th century and a vague sense that those were "the good old days."

EVERYTHING
NOT FORBIDDEN
IS COMPULSORY

SPORT IS ABOUT GOING FAST from A to B —
a phenomenon that has become more and
more evident in the latter part of the old
millennium. Yet we rarely stop to examine why
it is that we need to go so fast. Speed is an
aspect of life that finds its way even into drugs
— we must always get everything done at such
a rate.

But in the future, around the 26th century, it
may be that speed will take on a new aspect as
we find out what it is made from.

Zeno, the Greek philosopher stated that in
order to go from point A to point B we could
only travel in ever diminishing halves — that if
the distance between A and B is say 100
meters, the journey taken by the runner would
first be half of it — 50 meters, then half of that,
75 meters, then half of that, 87.5 meters, then
half — 93.75, then 96.88, and 98.44 and 99.22
and so on in ever diminishing fractions. In
effect, therefore, under Zeno's philosophy of
distance we would never get there because
there is always a diminishing half to be
covered. However fast you go there is no goal
and this is very typical of the original Greek
thinking because, although practically it has no
relevance, spiritually and aesthetically it is true
— there is nowhere to go because when you

reach what you imagine to be the end, you find
it was an illusion and you have to start all over.

Speed therefore may undergo a history of its
own in both directions. It is supposed in
theoretical circles, that the day will come when
we discover some particles capable of
traveling faster than light and perhaps even at
infinite speeds. Above the speed of light, of
course, speed becomes somewhat theoretical
anyway for we cannot "see" the traveling
particle with light any more — it is moving too
fast.

At the other end of the scale we may find
that everything very much slows down during
the centuries between now and the 26th, with a
resurgence of the importance of speed
occurring, as life becomes more difficult once
more during the Dark Ages of the 26th century.
In the motion picture E.T. and in several other
of the science fiction movies today,
transmissions are made over vast distances
without seemingly any delays. E.T.'s "phone
home", even to the nearest star would have to
travel on carrier waves at around two thousand
times the speed of light to get there in a day!

Very new research into the use of strange
sub-atomic particles called *tachyons* is already
happening in the 20th century, though tachyons

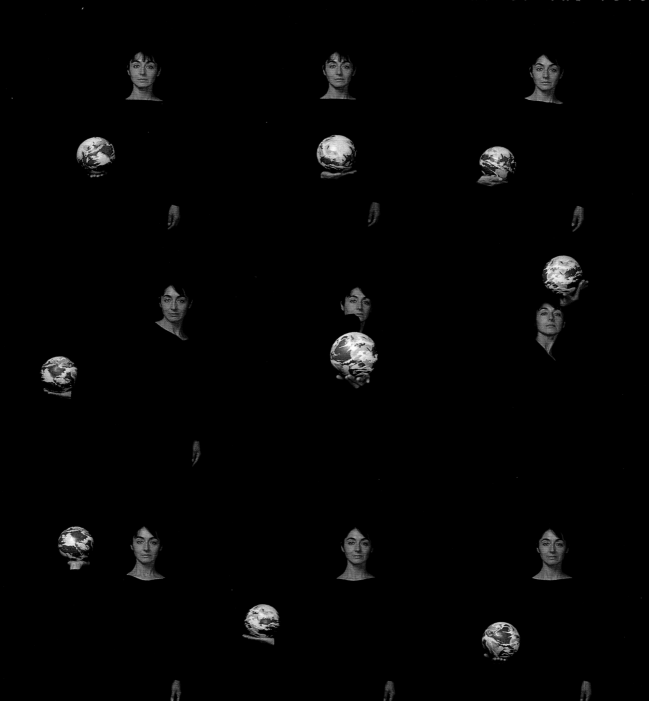

themselves have been around in the minds of scientists since the beginning of this century when the technologist Richard C. Tolman suggested they could be used to travel backwards in time.

Based on the premise suggested by T.H.White that "Everything not forbidden is compulsory", physicists are becoming more and more fascinated by these particles because they have not been forbidden by any of the existing laws of science. They do not go against, at least theoretically, Einstein's laws of relativity for Einstein only stated that anything which travels slower than the speed of light cannot travel at light speed or beyond it. Tachyons are thought to travel *only* faster than light. They cannot travel any slower and would never be able to travel at any speed except faster than light.

In this sense, then, they are like a mirror of everything that travels slower than light for the energy needed to speed something to the speed of light is as great as the energy needed to slow down the tachyon to the speed of light.

Tachyons are tough to prove, however, for they can only be detected by existing measuring techniques and these, during the 20th century, function with too many variables for certainty.

The implications of the arrival of faster-than-light particles move quickly into the realms of science fiction. Take a practical example — if we can plant a message onto the back of a tachyon and send it to Alpha Centauri — four and a half light years distant — say at 187,000 miles per second — the message will arrive just under four and a half years later. An answer would therefore be received, theoretically, nine years after transmission. This works fine over such a distance. But if we use the same message technique to any of our local planets, for example, the logic ceases to apply for the message on board the tachyon would theoretically arrive at its destination *before* it was sent. We would receive our answer before

we had asked the question!

In a short story written by Brian Aldiss, the British science fiction author, entitled *The Six-Minute Man*, the entire dialogue of the hero is written in reverse, with answers coming before questions, as the man in the story lives six minutes ahead of everyone around him.

Such dilemmas are presently not the subject of scientific research but by the 26th century they may have to be considered for here we enter quite clearly into the realms of time travel.

It seems that the basic problem of such reverse-time systems lies in the very foundations of our appreciation of time itself. We measure time according to light. We figure our year according to the speed at which we move about the local system, our months according to the lunar orbit, our days according to our appreciation of the sun's changes. All these time factors are based on what we "see" within our own heavens.

If we cease to see in this way because particles move at a speed faster than light, then perhaps we will need to adjust time itself and begin to look at the local universe according to another form of time-awareness — a much faster form.

Yesterday will no longer be something that has happened and gone — it will be something we can repeat! Today will be made up of several presents, some of which will be in the past, and tomorrow will arrive on our doorsteps at varying moments, some sooner than others.

This understanding of time already exists in areas of life constantly being experienced. When we are closely studying some important event — something which requires great concentration, time seems to pass more quickly, and when we are bored, with nothing to do, the hours seem to pass more slowly. It may be that such experiences are connected to different *actual-time* states. Deja vu may be an example of the yesterday/today syndrome described above, where events seem to repeat themselves as though they had happened exactly as they are presently happening. Perhaps we receive tachyon messages more often than we realize.

In the 26th century then, clocks and watches would contain not only a regularized time aspect, which would be operated to continue an "appointed" day movement — on a sun-setting aspect — but they would also contain "tachyon-time" variables which would account for double-presents, past-pasts and pasts. The operation would take some getting used to and presumably would work as a computer controlled methodology, bionically attached to our perceptions. The compu-brain would interpret the incoming data according to the type of particles carrying the message — whether they be light particles or faster-than-light particles. The interpreting mechanism would need to know the difference as the basic diagnosis format, and then apply the time pattern that was appropriate. Our conversations will then contain sentences such as: "Thank you for your communication in answer to my request, which I now transmit"! A topsy-turvy world awaits us in the future.

CENTURY 7

2600-2700

SOMETHING
MISSING,
SOMETHING
FOUND

And after any Dark Age
can come a Renaissance
— a return to magic
and miracles.
But perhaps this
time round we will
take the right turning.

	EARTH-NATURE	BODY-COLOGY	PHILO-THINKING	CHRONO-LOGY	PARA-SCIENCE
2600 • 2610		**BODY BUILDING** Youthanasia and new ways to create test-tube bodies.	**SIMULOGY** From dust to life and back again.		
2610 • 2620	**THE TRUE ESSENCES** Witches, channeling and the dark side of light.			**THE NEW CLOCK** Time-pieces that tell a hundred different times.	
2620 • 2630	**MAGICOLOGY MIRACOLOGY** The return of Merlin and the science of magic.		**THE SCIENCE OF ILLUSION** Discovering ways to make the invisible.	**MUSEUM OF THE IMPOSSIBLE** Future pasts collected for future futures.	
2630 • 2640					
2640 • 2650	**DOWN-TO EARTH** Finding practical ways of beating pollution.		**THE POWER OF THOUGHT** Brain trusts, brain storms, brain waves.		**THE COSMIC MIND** Thoughts and memories from cosmic sources.
2650 • 2660		**THE PLEASURE SEEKERS** Barbarella had nothing on this.			
2660 • 2670					
2670 • 2680		**FANTASY ADDICTION** Manufacturing the newest drug of total pleasure.			
2680 • 2690				**TIME-DIVINING** Tools to pick up new dimensions.	
2690 • 2700		**EARTHING THE BODY** Earth to Earth, ashes to ashes, body to dirt, dirt to man.			

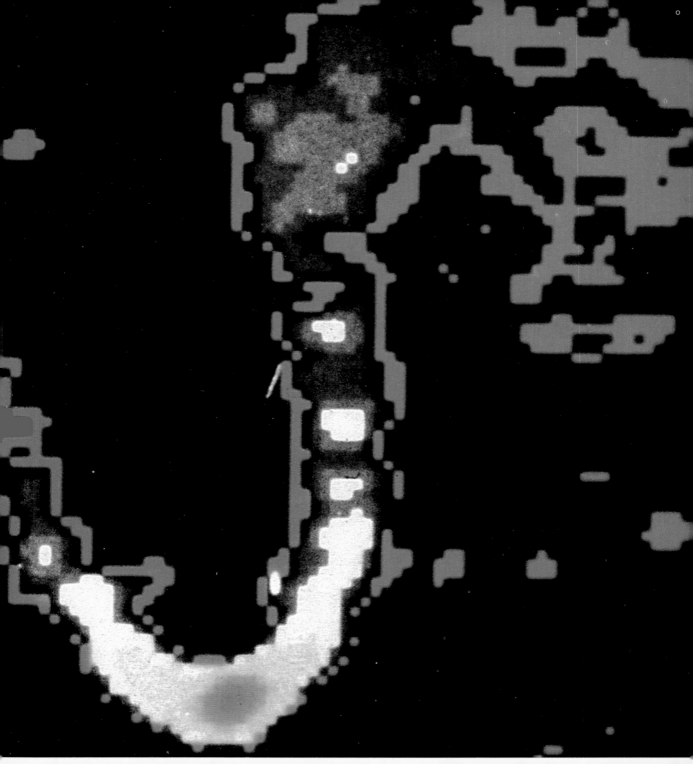

the miracle of holography but no doubt one day we will destroy this extraordinary aspect of life as well — in the interests of financial advancement.

Perhaps the greatest miracle of the future will be our realization that life itself is a miracle.

There are alive today, of course, true miracle workers — rare and strange people who can manifest a kind of reality that defies all rational understanding. One such is the guru Satya Sai Baba who lives with thousands of followers in an ashram in India. Before the eyes of crowds of people he commonly produces Swiss watches from nowhere and gives them to followers. Amongst his more familiar tricks is the constant manifestation of a kind of white ash that appears from his hands and pours in apparently endless amounts everywhere he chooses.

There are no scientific proofs attached to such behavior and yet it has been documented and observed by thousands, not only from Sai Baba but from other living and past Masters of the East. The explanation, which derives from the East also, is that the human passes through levels of consciousness, seven in number, on the way from the base physical level — that of physics if you like — right through to the highest levels of enlightenment and transformation. And one of the levels on this ladder of growth is a psychic level where miracle working becomes possible. Most of the Masters, then, have been miracle workers at some time on their path to heaven, and some simply get stuck there.

But what can we surmise might occur in the future, once the scientific discipline encompasses some of the subjects which today are decidedly fringe?

Witchcraft, for example, will become an established science in the same way that astrology was in the Renaissance, when all forms of thought and conceptualization were regarded as legitimate (except perhaps black

magic which was contra-religion) if they had something to contribute to man's improvement.

We are moving rapidly in that direction at the end of the 20th century with new sciences being born almost every month. In the United States it is virtually possible to create your own faculty within a university simply by writing a paper on a subject that doesn't fit in any of the thousands of other scientific combinations. Even the *para*-sciences have now become common ground for consideration, whereas a few years ago they were cast out of the established circles as being flaky. There is too much going on to discard any part of it as flaky any more. In fact, it is almost now as though the established scientists have become the flaky ones!

We might then look at the new sciences of the 27th century, such as *Magicology,*

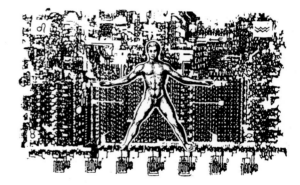

Divinology, and *Miracology* or give them all the general title of *The Science of Miracles*.

Much of the basis of such science will arise more readily if Sheldrake's and Bohm's proposals, expressed in the first chapter, are proven effectively. The presence of morphological fields will make it much simpler to understand that communication between humans, or between humans and animals or even between humans and inanimate objects, is perfectly possible simply because all these items of life share the same space in the

Divinology will be a sub-strata science of the overall Miracology and will contain experts on prediction, astrology, tarot, water divining and clairvoyance. Divinologists will be employed by the police as they are in a few special cases today, to track down criminals using evidence in the form of physical materials. They will also work closely with politicians to divine social trends and likely changes in political situations, and become involved in climate conditions, Earth-movements and general evolutionary trends.

The "scientists" who will be the qualified experts within these sciences will not undergo simply the equivalent of 20th century university education. There will be a need to supplement the old methods of normal learning, for it will be realized that much of magicology is derived from instinctive, un-learnable aspects of life. The adepts will become, therefore, apprentices to older magicologists and undergo long and deep cleansing of attitudes, social moralities and their absorption of spiritual understanding, before "qualifying" for the high priesthood of their particular coven.

There will be Master Magicians and Coven Queens who will command enormous powers to transform life but who will work within acceptable social standards to better the fate of mankind.

universe and are non-separate.

Magicology will contain what might be called the sub-science of *Intimate-Correspondence*, which may sound a little like a love letter, but actually refers to the sensitive process of communication on subliminal levels. The term intimate is appropriate because much of witchcraft includes a strong sexual element which derives its power from the female cycles within nature. A flourishing Magicological society will therefore need to have overcome its taboos about sex and death.

MIRACLES EVERYWHERE

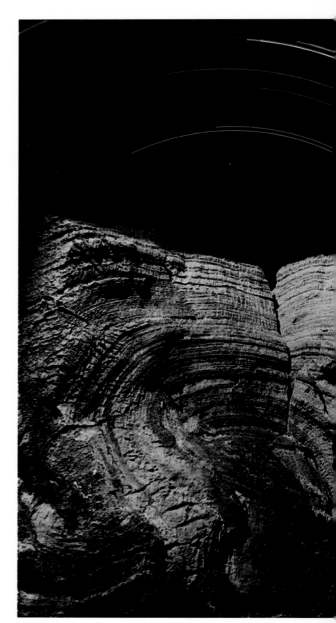

MIRACOLOGISTS WILL STAND at a higher level of the ladder of para-sciences with their capacity for manifestation but they too will be subject to the commands of the Masters themselves — the ultimate "scientists" on Earth — enlightened women and men who have achieved the final state of human intelligence and who will be maintained as government elders and advisors in positions of great authority and power.

All this may sound very unlikely unless we take a quick step back and look into the past. Not so long ago, in the ancient races of mankind such as the Egyptians, the Phoenicians, the Etruscans, operated much of their law through a kind of magic. This very special magic has become lost to us except in one particular area — our sacred places — the buildings, monuments and pieces of land often elaborately inscribed, which adorn almost every part of this planet.

Tombs, temples, churches, earth markings and many other even less recognizable forms, are scattered all over the world. Many of them mean nothing to us at all — at least not for sure. We debate the reasons for the building of edifices such as Stonehenge but we do not

really know.

As an analogy we could imagine a time, perhaps after a major holocaust, where all life and technology was wiped out on Earth. In this far-distant future, where technology existed in a different form from today, people might know nothing about our civilization and how it worked. The discovery of a radio or TV would be a great puzzle to these people. What does this small box do? The fact that we have elaborate broadcasting studios with complex entertainment programs carried to us by radio waves, to our little boxes might be missing, might be missing in their education of the past. This is roughly how it is for us and our most ancient past. Yet, in the far-distant future, a time may come again when the business of miracles and magic will become familiar once again and the still more ancient sacred places that we have today, will once again be used as they were meant to be.

The future may not only reveal more advanced forms of modern technology — the use of carrier waves formed by electrical impulse or transmission waves or even the most modern forms of fiber-optics — these things may become redundant in the face of much more subtle forms of transmission which derive from a deeper understanding of nature and her intrinsic communication systems.

Already today, we are faced with plenty of bizarre occurrences where people can "speak" to one another using what we call supernatural methods. It is likely that these new forms of contact will grow in their usefulness as we grow in our ability to merge with our environment. The Eastern religions have developed some extraordinary methods of staying in touch with one another. With the use of temples, alchemical practices, such as rubbing special oils into the skin, mantric sounds that create vibrations around the adept, they can make contact with one another on unknown and unexplained plains of life.

BODY BUILDING

Body-part warehouses will supply us with spares

By THE 27TH CENTURY it will be possible to have everything rebuilt. In fact you will be able to have your head, or your brain transplanted onto a new young body. The body will have been cultured from a single cell of your own body preserved from your youth. The subject might be called *Youthanasia*. Body parts will be taken from other bodies or grown in body-banks for exchange or simply vanity.

Artificial skin, test-tube skin, polymer nerve tissue, artificial bone made from very tough plastic, all are possible now. The problem of body-part rejection has been mastered to some extent by experimental part grafting, for example with a new nose, on the arm of the patient until the part is accepted by the body. The nose is then moved to its correct location once the acceptance is verified.

At the Los Alamos National Laboratory in America, scientists are already making *polyurethane* plastic bionic blood vessels that will be compatible with the human blood system. But the problem that must yet be overcome is that if the vessels are less than one quarter of an inch in diameter, the body coats them in cells and the blood cannot flow through. The attempts to create a plastic which will not register with the body as being a foreign object, seem at present the most likely answer.

First the polymer material is softened and then injected with a substance called *povidone*, a plasma substitute. The hope is that this povidone, which has similar properties to blood plasma, will fool the body into acceptance.

But all this is highly mechanistic and we have already decided that the distant future does not hold with mechanization. It is to be a time of magic and form-fields that can be manipulated rather like friends, not to be dominated by humans, but appreciated and accepted as part of a whole existence.

This theme will have registered in the mind of the reader of this book again and again. And it is a hard one to get away from once begun.

Imagine the patient being treated by a General Practitioner of the future, who will not resemble our own of the 20th century, for he will have learned much more, the

wisdom of life's magicology, has been apprenticed to a Miracle Worker, and to a Shamanic witch, as well as learning all the academic aspects of the body's physical nature. He or she has spent ten years in study and apprenticeship before coming to your body and the approach is nothing like that of the past or present.

The patient will be taken out to a nearby field where he will be "attached" to the environment by electromagnetic contacts which will create an introduction to Earth. The mother of mankind will take the primary position as healer and the Miracologist will act as catalyst or medium for this holy process of healing.

Any part of the body will be re-growable. There will be little question of replacing parts and if there is — if new parts are necessary — then the same system will be operated to manipulate or *affection* the form-fields within the environment of both the new part and the accepting body so that they combine in harmony.

Given time and practice such miracles will be workable, indeed normal. One happy part of all this will be the final goodbye to 20th century hospitals — places of human torture!

We saw earlier in this book, the plans of cryogenetic re-birth in which the head of the deceased is preserved in liquid nitrogen while the body is discarded in the belief that at some time in the future bodies will be grown and attached to the "old" and presumably cured head. The creation of a complete body is not beyond the bounds of possibility given both a full understanding of how the physical state of mankind occurs and an understanding of these invisible form-fields.

Given such a state in the far future there would be less reason for childbirth in the "natural" fashion. Couples might decide that they want to give birth to a child, simply through bonding and love aspects of the relationship, but much of birth would perhaps be taken up by those who do not wish to die. They would simply rejuvenate with a fresh corpus. The term "old-souls" might take on a new meaning in this case.

A CERTAIN ANTI-DEPRESSANT DRUG called *Anafranil*, medically known as a *tricyclic*, has been shown to have some interesting side-effects on patients taking it. When they yawn they have an orgasm!

In four well documented cases the users of the drug had spontaneous orgasm, whether they wanted it or not, while yawning.

Tricyclic drugs are known to have some strange side-effects but this one is about as bizarre as any and introduces an aspect of the future which may not be such a great surprise. Mankind will become more of a pleasure seeker than ever. This is particularly likely to occur at a time shortly after the predicted Dark Century between 2,500 and 2,600.

Chemical drugs have become a rather unhappy norm in the 20th century but with the refinement of a combination of natural and chemical substances, it will be possible by the 27th century to provide whatever kind of tailor-made pleasure the recipient requires, without any unnecessary addiction.

And much of this kind of pleasure stimulation will also be possible by direct implants into the brain itself. Even, eventually, the implants will not be needed for we will learn to "remember" specific pleasure experiences and thereby re-stimulate them again.

This particular propensity of the body has been observed by Dr. Robert Heath in his experiments with depressive and criminal patients at the Tulane University School of Medicine in New Orleans.

Patients are fitted with electrodes, sunk into the emotional centers of the brain — the *septal* region — where it is believed that the feelings of the body are governed. Angry and potentially dangerous responses of individuals can be converted into euphoric states by stimulation of these regions. The brain seems to remember past intake of drugs, for example, re-living the emotional and sensual experiences without the use of the drug itself.

The septal region of the brain is situated deep in the center of the brain under the frontal lobes and, shaped like a seahorse. It contains apparatus with some of the most exotic names in the medical list of human terminology — the *hippocampus* and the *amygdala* — almost Eastern in their styling. This part of the brain is considered to be the oldest in evolutionary terms.

The oldest portions of the brain may well be our source to many of the most fascinating aspects of life. If we learn ways of making direct contact with space and time in the manner suggested by the theories of David Bohm, we shall find that magic and miracles come neatly together with our fundamental existence.

The experiments being carried out by Dr. Heath entail low current triggering of the various emotions through the permanently introduced electrodes. The patients in question are schizophrenics, severe epileptics, people suffering from serious pain symptoms and other chronic sufferers. The effects of the probes is to bring about the various emotional states normally experienced by such patients in uncontrolled states but without the fear attached to them or the results. It is almost as though the artificial stimulation can produce the feelings without the disastrous consequences.

Heath believes that the root of schizophrenia lies in a defective pleasure system and an over-active aversion tendency so that the patient will more readily go into states of traumatic depression without the balance of pleasure to tip the tendency away. By stimulating the pleasure regions of the brain he has succeeded in diverting the problems of many schizophrenic patients. Whether this is the whole of the problem solved is unlikely for its

PLEASURE SEEKERS

methods seem to be as much rooted in the normal reductionist techniques of all 20th century medicine. There is likely to be a much wider and more holistic aspect to schizophrenia and other mental illnesses than can be dealt with simply on the basis of an electrical current in one portion of the brain. It is much like many medical cures during this millennium, striking at the surface of the problem rather than the roots.

Nevertheless the basic system will probably move into the future in the form of *Pleasure Machines* that can be operated at home through implanted probes or probes that can touch the brain's pleasure centers from the surface.

But there is a curious side-effect to all such medical research into mind-functioning human states — that of the "higher-state" of mankind which is still very much, as far as medicine is concerned, located in the cortex region of the brain. Animals do not much respond to the removal of this part of the brain, almost as though they don't need it at all, whereas humans lose most of their cognitive interest in, for example, the future or any form of higher knowledge. It is stated within medical and biological circles that animals are more in the "here and now" than humans and the 19th century physiologist Claude Bernard even made the statement that "In animals nothing is left to the ignorant will of the individual." It is as though science still considers a state of presence to be one of foolishness and the excessive presence of learning and information to be laudably that of the higher being.

By the 27th century we will finally understand that all aspects of life, whether "lowly" or "elevated" are termed in this way without meaning. We believe, during the relatively primitive 20th century, that animals don't even think — that their perceptions of life are without variance or individual choice and it is only in these very closing years before the next millennium that just a few fringe scientists are

beginning to wake up to the fact that animals have exactly the same potential response mechanism that humans have. They feel pleasure, they think, they decide — they just don't bother to tell us about it!

Pleasure and pain, then will grow into normal physiological capabilities in the next millennium without the shadow of any moralistic judgments. We will be enjoying vastly more leisure and our activities in life will be far more oriented to personal needs, spiritual growth and more esoteric pursuits. What is now slightly disparagingly termed "the me generation" will have become the normal generation as we realize that the understanding of ourselves is the primary need before any philanthropic or social fulfillment can be achieved.

We will not have vacations for all life will be one big break. The individual will have a complete internal knowledge of how the body works and will adjust and control the personal homeostasis by a subtle and complete intrinsic harmony. Thoughts will derive from a deep

meditative space and connect with a cosmic environment, in touch with all human, animals and every other form of life so that movement through the years of physiological existence will be a constant awareness of everything that is happening around us.

Sensitivity to our environment will take far more subtle forms than are at present experienced. It will not be a matter of being conscious only of pollution, planetary conditions or the more macrocosmic aspects of life, but much more to do with the most refined and delicate states. We will feel how it is to be a tree, a flower, a planet. We will be touched by every event in our environment right from the physical pain of others to the pleasure of a sunset or the halo around a bright moon. These things will be the miracles and will contain the maximum effect for the pleasure seekers of life.

Life will then be a constant miracle, for miracles arise very simply from a heightened awareness of events and if we learn not to take anything for granted then miracles are all around us.

FANTASY ADDICTION

*Vacation
on a
Star*

ANOTHER OF THE MOST OBVIOUS areas of pleasure and pain is that of the dream world, both waking and sleeping. We spend much time in a state of fantasy and some theoretical scientists and philosophers such as Alan Watts, for example, would say that we are in a permanent state of fantasy for life exists only as a dream in which we go about our business fast asleep.

Fantasy may be seen as a kind of arousal mechanism that brings us out of the everyday states of living, in which perhaps we feel bored or stuck. Fantasy supplements. In some it becomes an addiction.

We may see, during this latter half of the next millennium, a propensity for excessive fantasizing, perhaps in the form of very high risk activities or in the use of non-stop entertainment or self-created dream states. Increased leisure can bring about such occupations.

At the University of Wisconsin, studies have been undertaken to look at the whole process of arousal as a human factor. The central subject of the studies have often been those who continuously take very high risks in pursuits such as truck racing or sky diving. Subjects studied appear not to be much affected by the normal everyday stimulations that the rest of us enjoy. One might say that they are basically what the English term "thick" or "thick-skinned", or in other words unable to feel very much unless it is so grossly overstated that it is rather like thumping a flower with a meat cleaver in order to make it smell! Such characters are termed "Type T" personalities and apparently form some 24% of normal society, in varying forms. Not all Type Ts are so wildly risk taking as implied above.

The general view of such people is that they are in need of constant stimulation on such a high level because they have been conditioned that way since childhood. The opposite state is even less desirable — the Type t — which is the sort of person who prefers to live a secure and risk free life without any danger (Big T, small t).

It may be seen that in fact the state of excessive need for arousal stimulation at high levels, may be something else again. If we consider the constant activity factor involved in risk-taking as an avoidance technique, it becomes something new. We all operate to some extent in this fashion for we are all much afraid to face ourselves and our own personal failings and successes. But by the 27th century the emphasis on self-knowledge will have reached a far greater level of importance and therefore constant self-avoidance will be regarded as an undesirable state — even a sickness or an addiction — an addiction to fantasy. The risks and stimulations of the miracle of normal existence will teach us that we do not need to booster our normal lives with other activities if we simply stop and look at what is there under our noses.

And as the next millennium moves forward towards its last centuries so such awareness will lead mankind inevitably to higher and higher states of consciousness.

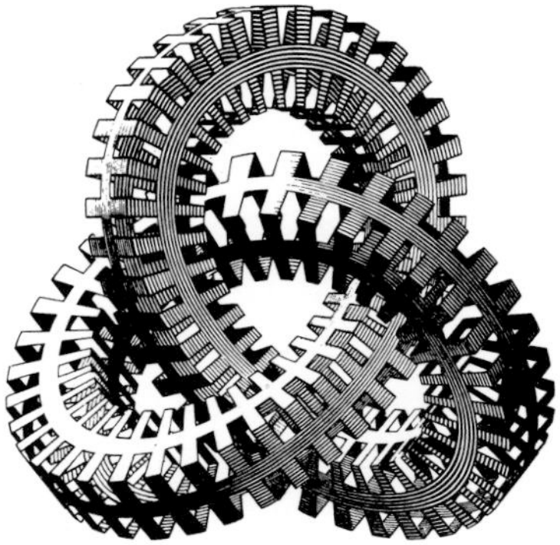

THE SCIENCE OF ILLUSIONS

ANOTHER NEW SCIENCE of the 27th century will be created out of illusion, we might call it *Simulology*, and for sure it has already begun in the 20th century with the TV and video world and the promise of holographic simulation.

Interactive laser discs already produce a sharp image with an instant game-change facility. This means that the response of the player in one of the new games is instantly placed in the game, so that the player effectively dictates the story line. Sound chips can listen to instructions and respond in audible language and the design of the games gives a clear three-dimensional effect.

Telephone companies in the States will this year provide video games over the telephone line to link directly into the home computer. The game industry has become so popular, especially in America, that it is taking greater leaps than many areas of technological innovation. We need to play in this serious life, though it is doubtful that television monitors will eventually be the form of that play. There are inherent dangers in too much exposure to the physiological effects of television rays and before so very long the process of true four dimensional games using holograms will outface television and avoid the risky side effects.

The speed of growth of the home video game technology is truly breath-taking. Less than fifteen years ago the very first coin-operated video machine was installed in a California bar and now we are seeing home video games easily as sophisticated as anything in the coin-operated market. Before the end of this century, to say nothing of the 27th, we will be seeing holographic games that display right in the middle of your living room in full dimensional reality. By the 27th century, though, or even well before, it is likely that entertainment systems will have taken on what might today seem wholly sinister aspects — as will shall see.

The likely technology to be applied to any home entertainment is the laser disc. For those who haven't seen one it is a silver-colored disc the same size as the long-playing disc and can retain up to 60,000 video frames or about half an hour on each side. It works in the same way the compact discs do — i.e. it spins fast and has a reflecting laser beam on its surface. The beam reads off the surface of the disc and "displays" what it reads either as sound or light or both.

The difference between the laser disc form of display unit and the computer graphics form is simple — the laser disc records actual video footage so that if the game contains a battle

scene or contains people, they are video shots, not fake shots. The laser disc system also moves fast enough to respond to human interruption and the laser can shift to another part of the disc and change the pattern of the story line in the game almost instantly. This and the video aspect give realism to the new technology.

Graphics are then superimposed on the video shots as well as stereo sound so that the ultimate effect is very realistic and if we have access to a vector-graphic monitor we can also use the 3-D games.

Voice recognition and response are already incorporated in a single chip produced by Milton Bradley.

All this, projected forward a few hundred years will be more sophisticated than we can possibly imagine — that is if we are still then interested in games at all.

Holographic-type games will be operated in the 27th century through direct brain link-ups in which thought patterns can be detected by the game machine and visualized four dimensionally. It will not be a matter of complex technology reproducing a fake version of the pre-recorded video game feature. The game will emerge directly out of the player's mind and into a scene right there in front of him or her.

The game will be playable as the thinker thinks — or in other words, the player will be both in the game and will create the game

himself — rather like a waking dream. There will of course be considerable dangers, for the dream-game will interface and interact with the players so that normal human responses will operate. If the game entails a battle in the wilds of Africa with a lion or a battle-field in which the player flies a Scramjet into a galactic war, the action will take place as very little different from the real thing. There may not be the physical presence of alien invaders but it will seem to all the physiological responses that there is!

Such games will of course also enter the risk factor of life which we have already looked at in the sports section of this book.

The playing machines would operate on more sophisticated designs than ever we can imagine today, but even at the end of the 20th century there are already plans for *Grope* harnesses which are similar to the bio-feedback systems already in existence. The control system would attach to the body and give all the sensory feedback instructions necessary for playing the game. The hands would experience the true feelings of the experiences within the game, such as climbing a mountain or swinging from trees or even touching monstrous adversaries, and the heart beat or pulse change would register as part of the players involvement in the game thus producing different responses in the illusory parts of the game.

MUSEUM
OF
THE
IMPOSSIBLE

T HE 27TH CENTURY WILL STILL, no doubt, reflect some interest in preserving the past. Museums of technological, archaeological and perhaps historical events will exist for people to sample how it was to live in the 21st century and beyond. Just as today we look back at Egyptian mummies and Elizabethan costumes with amazement at how different life was then, so the people of the future will stare at our strange fashions and the "quaint" ideas we have about life.

To us now, though, a museum of the past in the future will look like a museum of the impossible, for it will contain items that we could never in our wildest dreams figure out.

Old-style trains that travel at thousands of miles per hour will feature as outdated. Aircraft that use hydrogen atoms for fueling will also be obsolete. Alien beings with whom we have had brushing experience in the past and have lost touch with, will appear as holographic, moving records.

Such museums might even contain steam engines that would be our own heritage and perhaps examples of the internal combustion engine in the form of a Cadillac or Buick car from the old America — now a disbanded continent forming part of the World or Galactic Federation of nations!

Features will certainly contain biological phenomena which we might not wish to encounter, such as the likely mutations brought about by a nuclear war, or failed genetic engineering attempts during the times when science finally figured out that it is not possible to fool with nature without sad consequences.

Vast holograms of the local galaxy would feature the holistic and homeostatic changes occurring in nature as they actually happen. The geographic museum of the impossible would have complete records, going back millions of years, which could be seen in full imagery, of the whole process of evolution so far. Depictions of man's ancestors and the conditions they lived under, would so realistic that we could even step into that period like time travelers and interact with the mytochondrial mother of mankind herself.

For the impossible is only constructed from our own ignorance.

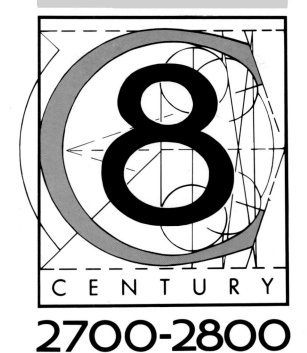

C8

CENTURY

2700-2800

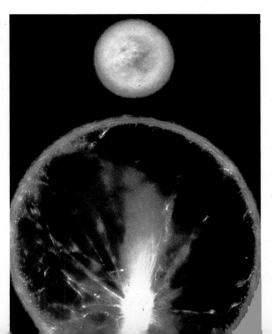

CHAOS
RAINS
BEFORE
MAN
LEAVES
EARTH

Fear-fields and the mastering of dis-ease. And as the universe opens up to the burgeoning magic of Earth, new influences enter from the "outside".

	PHILO-THINKING	MAN-SCIENCE	COMMUN-ICATIONS	ASTRO-NOMICS	THEO-SCIENCE
2700 • 2710	MEDITATION AND THOUGHT The power of the heart weakens the mind.				THE NEW DEATH A fresh way to look at the great taboo.
2710 • 2720		THE INVISIBLE BUILDING Solid structures can be reduced to forms also.			
2720 • 2730	FEAR-FIELDS — NEW DISEASE Sheldrake's Universal Habits expanded.				THE THIRD COMING A new Jesus Christ.
2730 • 2740			MULTI-PLANET COMMUNICATION Spreading our nervous system through the galaxy.		
2740 • 2750					
2750 • 2760	THE RAIN OF CHAOS After confidence the Fall has arrived.				
2760 • 2770					DIS-ORGANIZED RELIGION The new personal God.
2770 • 2780	UNDERSTANDING THE UNIVERSE Expansion along the lines of Marshall McLuhan.	TANHAUSER'S GATE *Blade Runner* comes of age.			
2780 • 2790	SEX TO SUPER-CONSCIOUSNESS Sexuality leads us up the ladder of consciousness.			SPACE-ROT Too much space to find the end.	
2790 • 2800					EXPANSION Opening up our awareness of life.

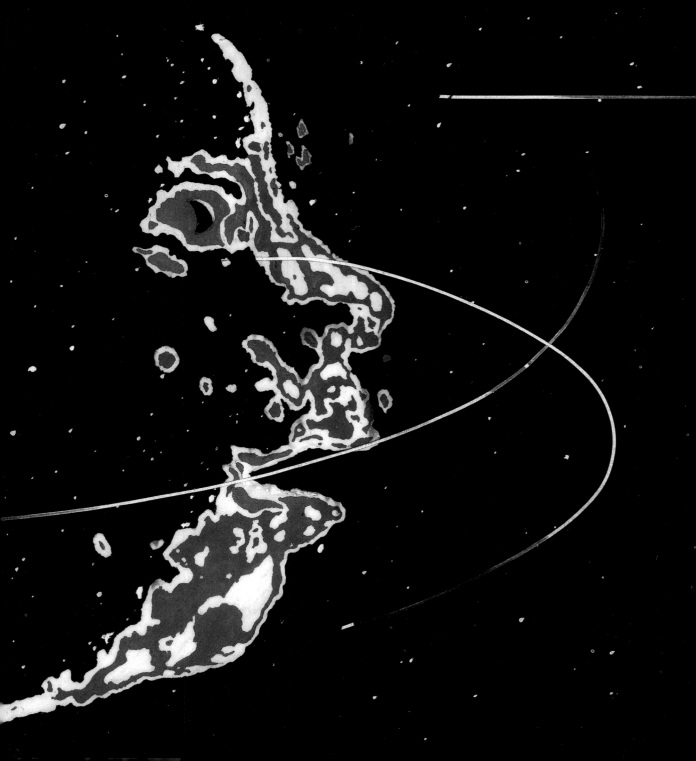

Breaking Away

2700 • CURING THE FEAR

How we can help to bring about our own diseases and how we can equally dispose of them — without medicine and without medical help

2750 • INVISIBILITY SEEN

As we discover that life is made up of invisible forces so we will begin to look and see them "appear"

2770 • SEX CONSCIOUS

Sexuality is seen as an energy in the future — pure and simple and without the taboos

2780 • SYSTEMS EXPAND

Marshall McLuhan believed that our communication systems were an extension of our internal nervous systems

FEAR FIELDS

THE WELL KNOWN AND POPULAR scientist Carl Sagan, has been called an exo-biologist for his interest and continued investigation into the possible existence of extra-terrestrial life forms. Mankind is always today on the look out for other types of life, intelligent or otherwise. And with Sheldrake's form-field theories uppermost in our futuristic minds, we may trace the chances of our own involvement in galactic presences, perhaps, with the idea of *Fear-Fields* in this chapter on the 28th century.

We shall also be looking at *AICS*, the new disease we invented in the last century, which wipes the cosmic memory, plus *Rains of Chaos, The New Death* and a *Third Coming*, and new systems of *Multi-planet Communication.* By the time man has reached a sufficiently advanced state that he can work with morphogenetic fields as an everyday part of his life, he will also have become aware of the full format of such a phenomenon — from the positive and the negative side.

We mentioned in passing the concept that, within what we can now call *The General Theory of Morphogenesis*, there exist form-fields which habitual provide order as it is. These fields also receive feed back from the environment and thus can be adjusted according to input. In other words, morphogenetic activity is the all and everything of life-forms and life-forms also contain morphogenic form-fields — they are interdependent and interrelating at all levels.

In this respect, we can look at a few practical examples of how life would be affected in, say, the 28th century, by such knowledge, proven conclusively.

The Invisible Building — given the full understanding of the fields themselves which

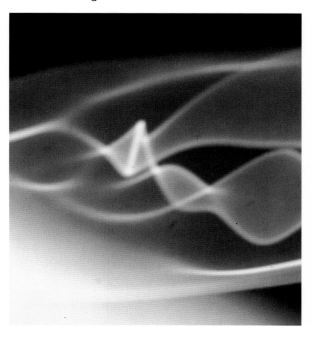

THE
NEW
DISEASE

habitually manifest physical forms, it would be possible also to create the fields *without* the physical forms. We would therefore see, or rather *not* see, buildings without any walls, floors, windows or roofs, which could nevertheless be occupied, entered and used in exactly the same way as physical buildings. The form-fields would create the conditions of the building without any need for the bricks and mortar! There would be some need for indications of the shape of the building, perhaps, or we might find ourselves bumping into walls or falling out of windows, but this could be done with artificial color codes present on different levels and positions of the building.

A more subtle method of detecting shapes in these invisible structures, might also be internal to the user. If we master and cooperate with forms, then we might also be aware of them ourselves without the need to use sight as we do with "solid" structures. What we call solid today is merely a set of vibrationary magnetic stimulations which set up the corresponding response in our brains. All matter is vibrationary and not actually solid, so that it may be that in the future, when we get in tune with form-fields, we may re-arrange our senses in an evolutionary development which permits us once again to "see" the invisible.

Such techniques could theoretically apply to all matter around us — which of course we would be able to change at will so that if the building didn't look right after a while we would alter it simply by changing the form-fields.

The other side of the coin will be the *Fear-Fields* which will be recognized earlier in the next millennium to be responsible for diseases such as *AIDS*. The fear-fields generated by anxious and disturbed social conditions such as over-work, stress, emotional unhappiness, sexual repression, sexual deviation, religious insecurity — result in form-fields which disrupt the human condition internally — i.e. they

create a disease such as *AIDS* or cancer. Once the disease has been recognized, the form-field's internal formation becomes a fear-field because the humans involved in the disease add further forms which include human fear. The fear-fields then bring further strength to the disease and it increases. The situation turns into a vicious cycle of events — each time the disease is re-emphasized by fear, so the field grows and the disease increases.

The realization of The General Theory of Morphogenesis will bring an awareness to medical science that the only way to cure diseases such as these is to cure the fear. The disease will then be made into something benevolent and will die a natural death.

In the 20th century such a concept, of course, sounds totally naive as we have no chance of recognizing, let alone altering the basic social disease which causes problems like AIDS and cancer, and we will therefore continue to suffer from such problems well into the next millennium. But by the 28th century a consciousness of new sciences and understandings may see such concepts realized.

Our new version of AIDS, named in the 27th century as AICS or Acquired Integrated Circuit Syndrome, will touch the human condition through the bio-chip technology of the time and eventually move in and damage the whole morphogenetic form field of our cosmic memory.

Perhaps man's need for disease also has to do with a conspiracy with nature which demands the occasional reduction of population at times when we are growing too fast.

Whatever the reason for disease there seems always one common factor that we need to learn about — fear itself. For fear-fields will be recognized as non-existential aspects of life — fear as a bottomless, self-perpetuating anti-force which feeds on itself and gobbles up mankind's naturally positive and enlightened nature like a large black hole.

THE RAIN OF CHAOS

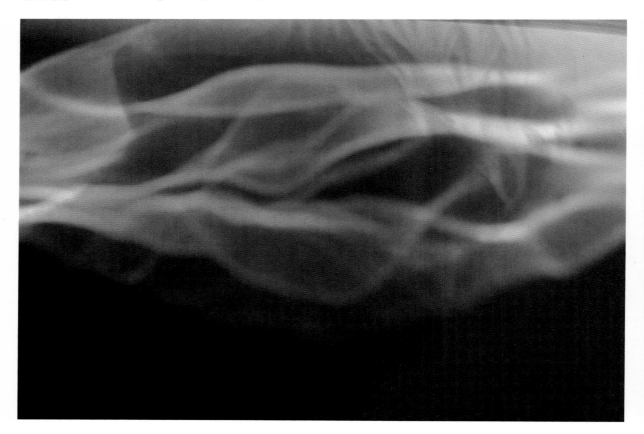

WE HAVE NOW STRETCHED OUT so far into the future that we are entering realms of prediction which border closely on science fiction. We may see, in our new form-field awareness, the Rains of Chaos, as the unidentified fields that stretch back millions of years, manifest themselves. This will include all the past events that have been lying dormant for millennia, such as dinosaurs, early man, even perhaps visiting aliens, all of whom left their mark on the morphology of Earth. These fields will open up and become perhaps manifest again in a chaotic period of long dead memories.

But, so as to bring us squarely down to earth once more and not get too much up into clouds of fantasy, let us return to more normal human elements — sex for example!

FROM SEX TO SUPERCONSCIOUSNESS

WE MAY CONSIDER THAT SEXUALITY must always remain the same — after all it takes two people, certain physical and emotional, chemical responses and the required location and there it is! However, on the contrary, there is likely to be a lot more to sex than that — hopefully!

Take the Cherokee Indians, for example. Quodoushka seminars, taking place in Native American spiritual sexual workshops during the 20th century, have shown that with "fire breathing" — a form of Kundalini energy exercise — it is possible to sustain orgasm for up to 45 minutes by bringing the breathing from deep in the base of the spine, the sex center, to the surface.

The lessons of Quodoushka have been held only in secret by the Sacred Council of the Elders of the Cherokee Indians, up until recently, but have now been revealed to non-Indians by psychologist Harley Swiftdeer.

The Cherokees use and teach the conscious application of sexuality for achieving higher states of consciousness. They state that there are five levels of orgasm, each with different sensations that can be practiced and learned with the Indian techniques.

Other Indians, this time from the East, have been saying similar things for centuries, and by, the latter half of the next millennium it would seem likely that we will have learned a good deal about Eastern techniques, especially as we are already seeing much interest in Eastern philosophies.

In the ancient Indian continent the practices of the seven chakras have been a central part of the pathway to enlightenment in the beliefs and performances of the Tantric religions. In these understandings of man's and woman's sexuality there are seven levels of energy —

which rise from the base chakra at the genitals — the bottom line as far as sexual energy is concerned — and the level that most of us exist on most of the time — right up to the head, where enlightenment can explode through the "uncoiling" of the "serpent" of chakra energy.

The Tantric followers practice some pretty bizarre activities, associating sexual energy with death, and performing, amongst other things, their sexual rituals close to graveyards. The association of Tantric energies with the female "yoni" developed many thousands of years ago when woman was supreme over man and was held to be the provider of the essential depths of life. Man could not achieve enlightenment without initial contact with the woman's sexual organs from which life, after all, derives.

In the latter centuries of the next millennium we may experience a rebirth of these ideas and religions, as we have already seen that woman takes a supreme position in matters of many of the areas of life presently occupied by man alone.

Sexuality will also see a growth pattern which is already being suggested during the latter years of the 20th century by the Master, Bhagwan Shree Rajneesh. Although Rajneesh may have gathered some unpopular views around the world, his basic message of love and human understanding does form a very sensitive and natural appreciation of the forces inside relationships.

He states that until we have learned how to love ourselves and our normal physical energies, we cannot hope to move up the ladder of consciousness. His book *From Sex to Superconsciousness* provides a clear understanding of how the human body works and how we can learn to relax our tensions through meditative processes. Many of his meditations may seem advanced and perhaps

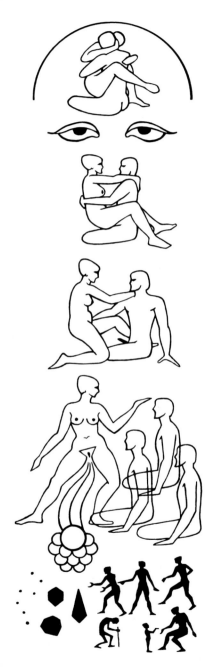

even disturbing, but their theme is always the understanding of physical and sexual power. He has gained the name of "sex guru" from his early teachings to his disciples in which various therapeutic methods were employed to free-up moralistic attitudes to sex, which Rajneesh states are harmful in the long term to all man's basic social rules. His ideas include the total disbanding of the institution of marriage and its rather archaic belief structures, which he says are attached to organized religions whose intentions were only to trap man into adherence to the particular dogma.

Given a more enlightened attitude to relationships and the foundation of love as the binding force, many of the old mores of life will disappear and people will remain within the loving forms of marriage which do not depend upon contracts and church rulings. Families would then be made more often of larger groups of people where relationships will be looser and children will have the benefit of a wider area of influence rather than being confined to the four rather claustrophobic walls of the nuclear family.

AND FROM SEX WE TURN TO the other most powerful of man's taboos — the existence of death as the final fear.

By the 28th century there will have come the realization that all parts of the universe merge together in a constant renewal of life through death. Many Eastern cultures maintain the concept of reincarnation in which man contains a spirit within his body which is non-physical, and which rises out of the body once the physical death has taken place. This has been a belief structure for many thousands of years and has become a popular idea during the 20th century also in the Western hemisphere, particularly amongst those who follow and support The Human Potential Movement or The New Age. In the Hindu religions of India, reincarnation is closely attached to concepts of karma in which we move from one life to the next "repairing", so to speak, the ills we have caused in our last lives. We are in this respect then, if we believe in karma in this form, prisoners of our pasts.

A new face in the Eastern

THE NEW DEATH

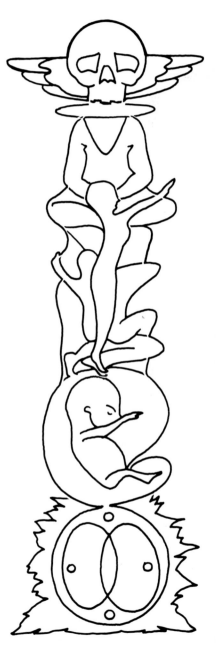

world — a Master who became somewhat visible during the late 1980s — named U.G.Krishnamurti (no relation to J. Krishnamurti) has proposed something still more advanced. He states that there is no spirit, no reincarnation, no karma in its present form — there is only the body — the physical body, and this body deteriorates and dies and becomes the earth once more like the flowers and the trees and everything else that exists on the planet. The cells of the body merge with the earth as they rot and they are reformed into something else in time. This way our bodies are spread throughout the planet surface and can become separately involved with trees, flowers, rocks, water or air. We literally spread out and are reborn as something else completely different.

The person who dies and becomes, in some part, a crop of wheat or a fruit on a tree, is then eaten by another human and becomes perhaps involved in the reproduction of a new child through the ovum of a woman or the sperm of a man. In this way the cells that died become new life in human form having passed through other life forms.

The concept then of physical rebirth without spirit may seem to us today rather depressing. We don't therefore get a chance to come back as another person in similar form with some considerable similarity in character. But we arrive back through many diurnal processes as though we have been consumed and digested by the earth and then regurgitated into human life — or many human lives.

Perhaps in the coming future we will discover that life and death are a mixture of both processes — spiritual and physical — in which the spirit of the body rises and rejoins another human being while the body breaks up and disintegrates into plants flowers and vegetables! It's all part of the cycle of life and death, after all, and in the 28th century you, the reader might find yourself living out this prediction as a reprint of the book you are reading now!

THE THIRD COMING

ERIK VON DANNIKEN SUGGESTED with some exciting, but somewhat circumstantial evidence, in his book *Chariots of the Gods*, that mankind may have been visited on more than one occasion by alien people who brought innovations to this planet which altered our destiny. Danniken proposed some fascinating and lateral ideas about various of the ancient edifices and earth-markings that are scattered across this planet, such as the cave paintings, the great white chalk drawings on British Hillsides, which he suggested may have been influenced in some cases by off-world visitors. A more recent and serious study entitled *The Genius of the Few*, opened up further discussion on the subject but it relates specifically to The Garden of Eden and the Genesis story in the Bible.

The author, Christian O'Brian, in this fascinating study, bases his hypothesis on Sumarian stone plates discovered early in the 20th century, which contain evidence of the stories of Adam's descendants. They point towards a small group of very powerful and

Although O'Brian does not directly presume that the beings were necessarily aliens from another world, the deductions point in that direction. The head of this enlightened family seems to have been taken as God himself by the lower humans and the powers that he displays are truly those of a super-being. There is even reference to The Tree of Knowledge of Good and Evil and this Tree of Knowledge carried fruits which were forbidden to the subjects of this great Lord but eaten by them anyway.

The creation of a new kind of life occurred during their rule on Earth and much of the interpretations given in the book are very close to the story of the seven-day creation and many of the other events that surround the Bible's telling. But the most exciting thing about it is that it all has much more of a ring of reality than does the Bible story of the same period.

We may presume, through our understanding of the modern interpretations of the life of Jesus Christ, that he was simply an enlightened Master who went through what is now known to be familiar processes of growth to a higher state of consciousness. We may take it therefore that concepts of heaven and hell, the old attitudes towards a wrathful devil and a super-human God, are to disappear with the age of enlightenment and knowledge — that we shall in the future no longer think in these terms but simply that we contain God in a more practical form than the Old Testament had it — i.e. ourselves and our lives.

The possible presence or arrival of alien super-beings, however, may be something we shall see in the future, and it may be that such arrivals will be regarded once again as the coming of God or the Son of God, at least by some. In any event, we are about due for another Godhead in our lives — the old one has become rather stale!

enlightened beings who lived at about the time of the stories in The Book of Genesis, and who controlled and ruled lesser humans in the Middle East. It is suggested that the Garden of Eden was their home and the great Flood portrayed in the Bible was a punishment on these people from their Masters. The flood itself, which is told in the Bible as being a devastation over the entire planet, is seen in O'Brian's book as only effecting a relatively small valley in the Middle Eastern region of the world.

TANHAUSER'S GATE

UFO's everywhere
The new World

At THE VERY END OF THE MOVIE *Blade Runner* the lead Replicant character tells the hero of the sights he has seen and amongst them are the lights of *Tanhauser's Gate*, some imagined place from the considerable mind of the author of the original story *Do Androids Dream of Electric Sheep?*

Blade Runner, although not successful initially in the box office, is probably one of the greatest science fiction features ever made and has, in the years since its release, become a cult piece with those who appreciate such works of imagination. It is certainly one of the movies likely to survive into a distant future.

But the world that it portrays — specifically the Los Angeles of the future, with its chaotic and overpopulated streets, constantly flooded by rain, with insanity and murder clearly the norm, is not one that many of us would enjoy living in. The advertisements on the flying bill boards report "off-world" colonies and "better worlds" than the one that seems overrun by people who look largely to be out of Hong Kong Island.

The future will certainly hold the possibility of other new worlds and one of the main features of interest will be how to get to them. By the 28th century there may be, not only the movement of small groups of people from one planet to another, but if conditions have not greatly improved or if Earth simply cannot hold us all, there may also be mass movements to other worlds. The way we in the 20th century would see such mass movement of humans, from one place in space to, another would be by human freight carriers with small ferries taking "bus-loads" off Earth to satellites and half-way stations. Passengers will get on board gigantic space vehicles that have been built in space simply because they would be far too big ever to rise off the planet's surface or get through the atmosphere.

But this may not be the way of it at all. The movement of the combined weight of millions of people in a space vehicle, would mean that the distances needed to be covered would never be accomplished, unless the passengers were frozen into a successful cryogenic state and slept the whole way there. By the time they got there the Earth would probably have burned out and there would be no coming back.

The other alternative involves using bio-computer storage of human cells, the formation and shape of which have been dis-integrated into their formative state, memorized by the bio-chip and then reformed at the other end. The broken-down bodies could then either be sent by carrier wave, like a sort of human telephone message across space, or they could be recorded on invisible morpho-discs which would be stored in formulated fields aboard a craft called "Starwisp".

Starwisp is the concept of Robert Forward, an American physicist and science fiction writer.

The craft will be a half-mile wide aluminum wire-mesh hexagonal — rather like a sail from a yacht, weighing almost nothing. The craft would contain some ten trillion wire intersections with tiny micro-circuits functioning as an integral computer network within the meshes — a bit like a brain but made of wire.

The propulsion would be achieved by a ten-

WIN
A
CRUISE OF THE
COSMOS
Trip for a Lifetime

gigawatt microwave beam which would be "fired" from a satellite in orbit around the Earth. The beam would be solar powered and work as a carrier for the Starwisp craft. The beam would focus on the sailship using a one thousand kilometer-wide lens positioned between Earth and the planet to which the ship was traveling. The ship would be capable of more than one-fifth of light speed and could reach the star nearest to us in a matter of a few years.

Although it is not specifically the idea of Forward to use the system for the mass transport of human dis-integrated cells, the possibilities are there, and in due time the craft could become the means of transporting human beings to other worlds.

It seems unlikely that we will manage to reach distant stars and planets by the methods that seem physically possible today, simply because of time factors and other material considerations, so that travel of such a nature will have to be formulated in new ways.

Another of the future possibilities is the existence of part-way stations. If we are to travel for years from one place to another, we are going to want to stop on the way for a break — re-integrate our bodies, have a coffee and sandwich and go on our way. Space travel will be exceedingly dull if there is no watering hole to pass the time in and exchange space-gossip about the latest galactic wars.

Plans already exist for what have been called "Galactic Grocery Stores" with provisions of water, fuel, hospital supplies and building materials.

The way-stations would be positioned in parts of space that have equal gravitational pull between two planetary bodies such as Earth and the sun — called *Lagrange equilibrium points*, and might eventually form a network out in space for travelers to stop and make connections for other destinations — rather like a down-town bus in New York City.

MULTI PLANET COMMUNICATION

WITH MANKIND SPREAD ACROSS the habitable universe, there will have to come some very effective communication systems. In the past one hundred and fifty years on Earth, communication has literally exploded into methods that would not have been conceived by anyone living in the early Industrial Age. And these changes, from the telegraph invented in the early 1800s, all the way up to the possibility of laser communications today, are the basis for what will bring the stars and planets together in the 28th century and beyond. It is likely that in a few hundred years, communication systems could well be as advanced by comparison to today's systems, as today's systems are advanced on those of the 1800s. But for our purposes in this book we can at least take a jump forward and try to envisage the growth of our "nervous system" through the galaxy.

The majority of space hunters looking out into the cosmos for friendly aliens, use micro-wave communications so as to avoid getting jammed up by all the other space noises there are around. But other theories propose that the use of laser light will be more effective for long distance communication.

Lasers are very narrow beams of light and can be very precisely focused on their target. They can also be aimed at very distant points without loss of transmission power. Additionally, the laser combines very high frequencies, with the greatest possible waveband-widths giving the choice of carrying giant quantities of information in one transmission.

Laser transmissions would also be capable, given the computerized dis-integration systems discussed earlier in this chapter, of "beaming-up" Scotty himself. The movement of information from one place to another might also contain the opportunity of moving people too. There might not eventually be any need to travel to the stars aboard a computerized craft. Passengers would simply be carried on a beam of light from here to where they wished to go, baggage and all!

Computers on the other end would unscramble the message and re-integrate the body that left Earth a few days, months or years before. Provided, that is, that there was no interference on the way! Such a system might need some very brave guinea pigs to iron out the glitches.

DURING THE 1800s, man had already begun to imagine that he understood the universe. This was an era of powerful advance both in science and industry with many men becoming rich from the new Industrial Age of coal mining and steam power. Science made some dramatic advances against disease and in the fields of physics and biology, even though perhaps since then much greater understanding has occurred. During the 19th century it was as though life had woken up to greater possibilities.

Perhaps the 28th century then will be yet another time of expansion, this time into the heavens and the worlds far beyond our present reachable distances. Almost a full millennium away we will find ourselves in possession of great skills that are unimaginable today.

What we can be sure of though is that the expansion of man will also mean an expansion of his conscious awareness of himself and his potential.

As Marshall McLuhen taught earlier this century, the communication growth of the electronic wiring of this planet is like an extension of the human brain across great distances.

By the last centuries of the next millennium our power to extend ourselves will have reached out beyond the material Earth and into the void of space.

But what will be happening back on old Earth?

How will it be for those that are left here — *On The Beach*?

C 9 E N T U R Y

2800-2900

THE
RAINS
OF
CHAOS
BLOWN
AWAY

If Earth remains
unconquered and
those in a rush leave
for other worlds, what
will be left on the
"Old Planet"?

A Quiet Earth

2800 • THOSE LEFT BEHIND

When mankind has largely drifted off planet Earth for new worlds, what will be left behind?

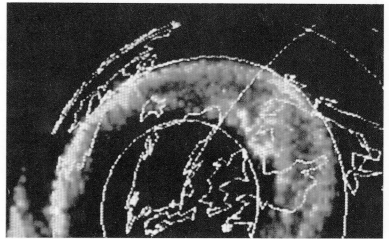

2840 • UN-SCIENCE

By the 29th century science will have grown wider and will encompass all the "para" concepts as realities

2850 • SPACE TIME

Infinity right now is something nebulous and forever, whereas in the future it will be shown as having definite boundaries

2890 • BOHM COMES HOME

Space folding expanded Matter transfer through direct contact with any part of the universe

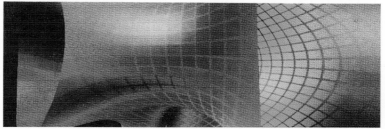

PHILO-SCIENCE
OF THE
LAST INHABITANTS

IN 2990 THE REMAINING INHABITANTS of planet Earth will look back at our times — at the 1990s and laugh. From that distance and the intervening learning, we will look a very strange and perhaps somewhat comic people with our struggling, our conflicts and misunderstandings of how life *should* be — taking ourselves so seriously and operating as we do, so much through our minds.

In the late 20th century, we have already found a flavor of newness in the spiritual New Age. The opportunities presented to us for silence and a natural harmony are there and yet we persist in our insistent and archaic assumption that the mind is everything. We constantly determine life according to a linear structure which depends upon reason and in so doing miss the truth by a thousand miles. We believe ourselves to be advanced and almost on the brink of *the final knowledge*, when the truth that has become evident from our brushing acquaintance with the East is clearly something totally different.

Perhaps, when those people of the future look back at us they will see our seriousness and fear and contemplate a time of chaos that was the beginning of a bridge to real under-standing. For by then there will be a philo-science in which science and religion will have become joined into one broad mind and spirit.

Such a combination of the two sides of life

will manifest itself, perhaps, in the elders who remain on Earth after most others with more urgent energy have left for further conquering and travels into the galaxies beyond our own. And those remaining will be a peaceful and meditative population who will build an Old Earth in the way that they wish. Population will be very low, perhaps less than five hundred million people with all cities disbanded except

perhaps central administration areas that will be composed of government and the organizational aspects of the world. The rest of the inhabitants will live in communal villages spread across the most beautiful parts of the land and water.

People will choose their lifestyles according to an intelligent method, harmonizing with Mother Earth, and no longer abusing her power. Communities will operate farmland for their own food and be largely self-reliant for resources and technology, with recycling methods of a very sophisticated nature. Power and energy will be taken from the wind, water and the rock and will be sufficient to sustain the lives of all who live off the land.

Religion will be something intensely personal and the occupants of the communal towns will number no more than two to three thousand in each area, though there will be constant interaction between communes.

Money will not exist at all and the needs of individuals will simply be provided without greed or ambition so that the stresses and anxieties of 20th century life will have vanished altogether. An attitude of mutual concern and love will exist among the people, who will create a progress based on individual growth and a raising of consciousness.

All this probably sounds, to the 20th century mind, a little utopia-like, perhaps somewhat cloudy and unrealistic, but in fact such a lifestyle will be very grounded and down-to-earth with an intensely practical aspect. For once the human mind learns that it is possible to operate through self-love, then all ideas of politics, war, striving and greed will disappear naturally. The unwillingness of many to taste the power of the Human Potential Movement in the 20th century arises only out of fear of change. To the remaining inhabitants of this harmonious planet in the 29th century, no such attitudes will exist.

In his book *The Awakening Earth*, Peter Russell surmises that if a group of say 1000

people sit together in one place and meditate, the energy that arises from them circulates the planet as a subtle influence and effectively alters the whole state of the world. The influence may not be consciously felt by the rest of the population, but nevertheless there is something that changes. The chaos and anxiety that is going on throughout the majority of the world also, of course, brings an influence, with the resulting energy also traveling about the surface and affecting everyone. It is this influence that most of us feel more readily than the peace and tranquillity coming from an ashram in India. It may be supposed, quite rightly, that the occurrence of dis-ease in the form of AIDS or cancer or any of the other major disquieting influences of mankind, arise most readily from that traveling influence engendered in cities like New York or London.

By the 2990s there will be monitoring machinery that will detect and take note of the changes of such influences , so that if a crime is committed or an act against nature performed anywhere in the world, the rest of the planet will know about it.

We could call such a machine a *Morphometer* and predict that its use will be to keep an eye on the changes and influences that exist on Earth. Each commune will have one, and the people living around it will communicate with one another so as to discover the negative influences and adjust them accordingly. Mother Earth will then be accepted as a living influence inside which man, the animals, plants, rocks and all other materials will be working together in an intelligent state.

Inside the homes of the inhabitants there will be large silent rooms. Each couple or family group will occupy their own apartments which will be high-roofed, naturally heated and circulated with humidified pure air. The furniture will be sparse and very comfortable with an emphasis on items that work to increase the resonance of a peaceful mind. Artificial entertainment systems will have disappeared as mankind learns to enjoy life simply by the benefits of his own senses. His surroundings will be rich and colorful and much of his time will be spent in working the land, with an emphasis on the physical connection with earth and the elements. All artificial life forms will have gone and the natural rhythm of day and night will be observed as a ritual — waking at dawn and sleeping soon after dusk.

Family life will be open and yet private and intense. All those living together will respect the other's privacy but also have access to one another without the awkwardness of dishonesty and false identities. Intimacy amongst members of the communes will be a strong aspect of living, though sexual intimacy will generally be confined to couples in bonding relationships.

The main forms of creative interest will be music and art and much of what is visible in the home will be in the form of morphogenetic artwork and form-music produced by members of the communities.

Every community will be headed by an *Enlightened One* who will be the teacher of the people and will carry through the traditions and understandings of the commune to the next generation, somewhat in similar form to the ancient Shaman.

In the administrative centers government will be by referendum with all matters decided through general voting. The central committee for organizing and implementing affairs of administration will be on a rota system with each oligarchic governing group standing down after one or two years of government. Those who take on the job will have reached their position through a meritocratic system, taking examinations and tests for capability. There will be no drama in government and no such thing as politics.

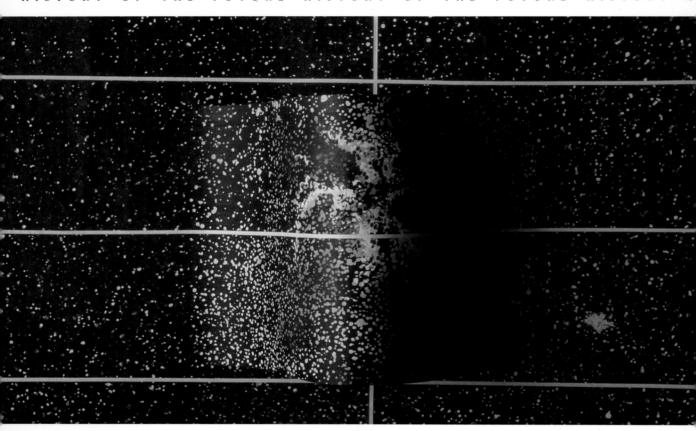

WE TOUCHED ON THE SUBJECT OF folding space earlier in the book and its relevance to David Bohm's theories of *Implicate Order* and the wholeness of existence, but we will again pass by this extraordinary and futuristic concept in its relevance to our new philo-scientific ideas.

It is of particular importance to our potential future insofar as its development will alter our entire perception of how the universe operates. If we can literally travel from our planet Earth to a planet on the other side of another galaxy in a matter of moments, many of the present ideas of linear space and time will vanish

without trace. This will again reinforce the new scientific frame of thought.

Put in practical terms, the space traveler who wished to visit a planet in the Andromeda Galaxy would make his or her way to a *Space-Folder* (which sounds a little like something we might find in a typing office) and take up a place in a small space craft. This would carry the traveler to an off-world satellite, the whole of which would be moving to the other galaxy. Using a form of computerized transfer unit which would contain matter transference computations to maintain the human frame in its precise shape, the satellite would gather up

192

FOLDING SPACE

Getting from here
to there
without moving.

an image of the planet to which it planned to travel. The computations would include surrounding planet influences, and would combine them with the exact same influences and forms of the area of space that it was leaving.

Space and time would then be combined in the holographic unit of space in which the satellite existed. A memory trace of the area of space time in which the other planet existed would be brought into the computation. The two would then be united by some means unimaginable by us. The holographic "plate" of the universe holds all the information for all parts of its own space time, so that taking the jump from one pattern of the plate to another simply means folding the two together in a new unfoldment of their positions. The satellite and its occupants would thus find themselves in a matter of moments, or non-moments, across the other side of the universe.

The concept of folding space can only be seen today as something wildly fictional but the shift from a linear appreciation of space time — i.e. something that moves from A to B in a fixed or varied time through past, present and future, to a more lateral approach in which time and space exist around us everywhere in every form and every moment, will open the doors to many new formats for life.

For those of us who have a problem envisaging what space-folding could possibly mean, there is a simple and practical method of indicating how it works right in the home. Though this example may not be the precise equivalent of something which today we don't even know the mechanics of, at least it brings the experience a little closer than straight forward explanation. Simply take a piece of ordinary card, preferably black, and cut it to maybe one foot square. Now dot the card all over with white spots — use a felt pen or white paint. This is your galaxy of stars laid out flat! Next fold the card exactly in two so that the piece is now half its size and double its thickness. Now take scissors and cut two cuts down either side of the middle of the card, both starting from the fold that you made. When you open out the card you will have a square cut from the middle of it except that the end of the square will still be intact. This you should then fold inwards. When the card is opened out you will have a kind of three dimensional card sculpture with one part of the card folded backwards and one part folded out forwards. You will see a rather more elaborate version of this technique illustrated in this chapter except that the artist who made the one for the book is a professional. Our way is a little simpler!

The resulting piece of folded card represents two things. If we lay it flat once more we have a one dimensional abstraction of space. If we fold it once, ignoring the cuts, we have a two-dimensional abstraction of space and if we pull out the cut folds and fold the central square forward, we have a three-dimensional abstraction of space. We can do all this with our hands and with one piece of card.

Now notice that when the card is folded into its three dimensional format the stars that were once far apart are close together. They are close together in a number of different forms. In effect, therefore, we have folded space. We have brought two different forms of matter together from being apart and the space that existed between those forms of matter have also been folded and brought together.

OK, so the methods for folding vast areas of the universe together may not involve scissors and pieces of card but the principle is not too far from the actual. We understand space to be something fixed and linear — from here to there — whereas it may actually be totally un-fixed and non-linear and easily flexible in terms of our movement in it.

Imagine a universe where we can travel anywhere through the infinity of space in a lifetime, where we can govern the timespan of our own lives, decide when and where we will live and die and what form our lives will take. There will literally be no limit to the power of the human being.

And this is exactly the essence of Nostradamus' last predictions. That mankind would overreach himself eventually and come to a sticky end. That the planet Earth would end far sooner than man expects, but that mankind would continue to live a life in other parts of the universe.

In our future time of the 29th century we are approaching quite close to that moment, and man will be aware of the possibilities of the destruction of this Home Planet Earth for he will also have the power to look into his own future. For the power to fold space also carries with it the power to fold time — the two go hand in hand, at least in this respect. The process of moving across space in timeless jumps creates some fascinating new thought patterns. We would no longer speak in terms of travel from one planet to another as being something involved in hours or years. The journey would be the same as passing from facing one way to facing another, without moving the body at all. We consider it normal to do this within our own small portion of space but to do it within a vast area of space seems ridiculous. Consider once again, then, the fact that upon a single holographic plate, the whole

image of the picture recorded exists everywhere on the plate — every spot of the plate is everything on the whole plate. Space and time can be seen as the same. But here we get too close to science fiction in our attempts to show the future. Though of course, compared with a hundred years ago, we are living lives of science fiction today. Especially in our new scientific and technological paradigms.

And while on the subject of science and science fiction we are going to take a slightly side-long look for a few pages, firstly at something that has gained a growing importance in the 20th century — astrology and *The New Astrology* of the next millennium.

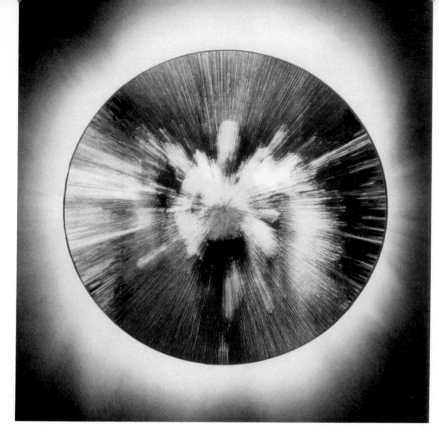

THE NEW ASTROLOGY
Space-time

THE "GREAT YEAR" IN ASTROLOGICAL terms stretches approximately two thousand years and forms a human era guided by the potentials of the astrological sign by which it is governed. The endings and beginnings of the different ages overlap by several hundred years and the age that we are now experiencing, the 20th century, is at the conjunction between Pisces and Aquarius, influenced by both water and air.

The Piscean Age was that of the Christian epoch and the Aquarian Age is occupied by science, humanity and learning, beginning, as it did in approximately the 18th century with the American Revolution and the Industrial Revolution. The year 2,000, our next millennial cross-over in time, is the point at which Pisces and Aquarius form an equal influence.

The great 16th century prophet Michel de Nostradame or Nostradamus, as he was popularly known, predicted that the Aquarian Age would continue until approximately the

196

end of the current lunar cycle — around the year 2250.

Aquarius turns man's face to the sky, to the frontiers of space and time and according to Nostradamus in his letters to Henry II of France, this will be an era of space travel and an awareness of the Home Planet as a whole world in which world government will provide a more balanced way of life. It is also a time when we will join the galactic community, when we will have the power of life and death in our hands and when we will literally know no boundaries in our powers to travel through time and space.

The people of the late "Third Millennium" will be as mighty giants if compared with us today and this, Nostradamus predicted, may also be the reason why there will eventually be a mighty fall.

Our challenge today, in the 20th century, is part of something very much bigger than we may imagine. Georges Gurdjieff, the early 20th century mystic, stated that there can be no true spiritual growth without an awareness that each moment may be our last. Within this era of the dying Pisces and the new Aquarius we face total death at the hands of politics and war. This may be our method of learning how to face death on a day-to-day basis — somehow giving us the booster we need to jump forward into a new era of life through harmony with one another and our world.

Nostradamus believed that if we manage to get through this time of trouble we will emerge into a great period of peace and understanding like no other on this planet.

"Before the moon has finished her entire cycle (1889-2250), the Sun and then Saturn (the Aquarian Age) will come. According to the Celestial signs the reign of Saturn will come a second time (Capricorn Age), so that all is calculated, the world draws near to its final death dealing cycle."

The progress of the centuries in this book has been approximately in line with Nostradamus' predictions that were written in his volumes "The Centuries" four hundred and fifty years ago, with a period of relative peace and growing consciousness during the first half of the next millennium followed by a fall from grace in the second half. But one distinct difference according to the great "Celestial Master" was his belief that the world would end sooner than ever our science tells us it will — namely in the 37th century after Christ — specifically in 3797 when he predicted the coming of a cosmic source of destruction with showers of meteors which would consume the planet completely.

Astronomy today functions as a sort of quasi-science, using mathematical and physical formulas which depend for their accuracy on the position of stars and planets. But in very recent years the planetary formations have changed radically and the presence of new planets, or at least suspected new planets may have altered some parts of the astrological conditions.

It is hard to be accurate with a scientific theory if you do not possess all the facts required to formulate the theory and the existence of the new planet "X", for example, believed to reside in our own solar system, may well change many aspects of the heavens for future astrologers. By the 29th century, therefore, astrology may have become a complete science as we shall be in possession, through precise experience, of all the information needed to map the local heavens.

Additionally, astrology may grow more popular and credible through the understanding that mankind's presence in the universe is not a separate one but part of the complete wholeness of life. Astrology would seem to fit well in this philo-scientific format.

One of the most dramatic changes, however, which we should see occurring, perhaps towards the end of the next millennium, is the incorporation into the science of astrology, of the whole concept already discussed of morphogenesis. If astrology is the study of the effects on people of the stars and planets then these effects must be generated through the form-fields that surround them. Each planet and each star has its own form-field — that which originally created the habit for its natural existence. Each human being is also surrounded by the influences and habit-memories of form-fields, and in between the stars and planets and the humans are further hosts of form-fields. Ultimately the philo-science of the 29th century will inevitably bring the two areas of influence together — the macro-science of planetary bodies and the slightly more micro-sciences of human potential. The form-fields that are generated around and between each planet and star actually help, not only to form the characters we so avidly read about in the newspapers and magazines under the horoscope sections, but more precisely decide exactly what shape, form and habitual presence each human being will live with.

The moment of birth, and likewise the moment of conception, occurs at a precise astrological time where and when planetary bodies happen to be moving within specific influences. These influences are formed by the morphogenetic fields and thus create the human frame, or help create it, to be in the shape that it is. The continued movement of the planets and stars then influences the moods and feelings, the processes of life and everything that occurs during the life span of that person.

These ever changing and developing fields of natural habit will become a major part of the future philo-science. We can expect to see sciences named *Astro-genesis* and *Morphastrology* whose studiers and experts will spend their time in precise predictions of the movements of planets and their influences on people, climate, Earth changes, future wars or other social conditions.

THE NEW ART

"Imagination was given to man to compensate him for what he is not; a sense of humor to console him for what he is."
Francis Bacon

ART IS AN ABSTRACTION of life. Its purpose, in all its forms, is to create something which represents man's view of his surrounding universe. It can never *be* that universe — at least not during the 20th century. But in the far future this may change. Art may become a reality experience — a form of life that *is* life itself.

It will be possible by the 29th century to create very easily, art forms such as wall pictures, that change with the mood of the owner. The colors, patterns and shapes of the art will be created with a kind of liquid crystal display which will reflect color and receive heat. A small chip will interpret the mood of the person in the room simply on the basis of the heat changes. There might be some interesting results during parties but at this early stage of the existence of "Mood-Art" who cares!

As the art of art becomes more sophisticated it will be possible for the picture to be holographic and exist as a self-defined whole in the room, hanging from nowhere in a kind of suspended state using hidden projectors to create the light needed for the exposure. Such "pictures" would need, at least to begin with, a holographic plate to carry the image which would be visible from all sides as though it really hung there.

A logical progression from still holography is moving holography but this will rely upon the development of some kind of film that can carry the holographic image and be projected by frames in a similar way to the old cine film movies. Alternatively there may be in the future

some form of computer simulated holography in which computer graphics manage to create the holographic effect and reduce it to an electronic signal which could then be stored on magnetic tape.

And here again we come back to the form-field potential for art. If man in the future can control and regulate form-fields there is no reason why we should not be able to create just exactly what we want in the shape of any abstraction, and ultimately, in life-forms themselves. Art would then become reality as we would find, in the future home, people and events actually being created by the rearrangement of form-fields.

On a more prosaic level we will see new arts such as *Living Theater* in which the audience will create their own plays by thought projection, *Instant Novels* in which the reader will project a basic fantasy into a computer

and the computer will write around the theme and print out, or screen a complete book.

Computer art is perhaps one of the fastest growing art forms of today as the little chip is now able to make the most fabulous illustrations.

The future will bring more and more sophisticated art from the computer with technology as its basis. Laser printers permit the very best reproduction of the art and soon enough we will be able to go to our lap-top and produce a fresh piece of art, print it and hang it on the wall in a matter of minutes.

The essence of all this is man as his own artist. Art in the past has always been the exclusive privilege of very talented people who then impress the rest of us because we could never do such things. But the day is not far away when art will in some respects become extremely cheap — hopefully only financially, and not in terms of quality!

THE PARA-SCIENCES

The most fringe sciences become mainstream.

T HE PSYCHOLOGISTS WERE THE first to put the prefix "para" before their title, perhaps because psychology, the study of the mind and its functions, is one of the least certain of human sciences. "Para" means "beside" or "beyond" or in some interpretations "wrong."

Originally it was perhaps intended to imply simply "unlikely" but today there seem to be so many para-sciences that we begin to wonder whether everything is becoming more and more "beyond." Certainly the idea of being wrong or unlikely is slowly dropping out of the picture of the para-sciences.

Now there is para-biology, para-physics and an ever growing number of beside-sciences.

It does seem at the moment to be a kind of transition title given to areas of science that are not quite understood. Perhaps, as they become clearer so the prefix para will be dropped and we will find parapsychological aspects of life integrated into simple psychology.

By the years of the 29th century the word para will either have disappeared altogether or become attached to the new, little understood sciences of that age. We may see titles such as para-archaeologists or para-evolutionists as these sciences become allied to religion and spiritual discovery. The whole realm of the Eastern studies, for example, as they enter our lives and become subject to "serious" study, might warrant the prefix.

Already today there are para-religious studies forming as the New Age spreads into the realms of channeling. Keeping our feet on the ground becomes more and more difficult as we apparently make contact with beings who died thirty five millennia ago and more.

Science, not unnaturally, views these studies with much suspicion for there is no hard evidence available for the scientist to grasp. The performances of active mystically oriented characters such as Uri Geller gave science at first a shock, for the bending of spoons and other metal objects seemed provable under laboratory conditions. Unfortunately the ultimate results were too much peppered with failure and possible fakery so that Geller and others have now been relegated to the scrap heap of the para-sciences.

There are numerous reports of large groups of people, usually in numbers of approximately twenty-five, apparently a magic number for metal bending, who get together and succeed in bending all manner of things simply through the exercise of the will.

Life continues to throw up such events but still without any clear proof that is satisfactory to science.

Perhaps the truth lies in the fact that laboratory proof is not the format for the para-sciences and we need to rethink some large part of our scientific methods to cope with them.

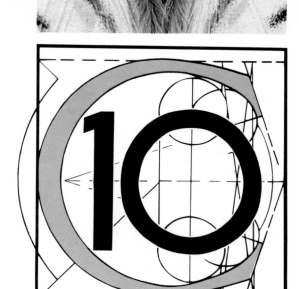

10

CENTURY

2900-3000

*END
OF
THE
THIRD
MILLENNIUM*

We could say that as this is the last century of the book that it should end on a positive note. But the world does not necessarily operate that way.

PHILO-SCIENCE	MAN-KIND	NATURO-LOGY	EARTH-NATURE	QUESTIONS-ANSWERS
2900 · 2910	**THE NOW AGE** Coming back to the present.			**THE FINAL ABSTRACTION** Sheldrake answers.
2910 · 2920		**NEWSPEAK** Future languages.	**GHOSTS OF FORM** The last vestiges of a life.	
2920 · 2930	**FASTER THAN LIGHT** The particles on the other side of light.			**FINAL MOMENTS** The author supposes.
2930 · 2940	**REMEMBERING GOD-THOUGHTS** The cosmic thought-field.		**MORPHOLOGY AND AIDS** Do we create our own dis-ease?	
2940 · 2950	**ANGELS OF DEATH** A new kind of dying.			
2950 · 2960				**WHERE DO WE GO FROM HERE?** Utopia versus death.
2960 · 2970				
2970 · 2980	**PSYCHICS IN EVERYTHING** Weird realities becoming normal			
2980 · 2990		**A FAMILY OF TREES** Talking to the oldest race on Earth.		
2990 · 3000			**ANCIENT LIVES** The oldest of the old.	

So Far So Good

2900 • SHELDRAKE

A few last questions put to Rupert Sheldrake bring some fascinating further proposals from one of today's most likely science-masters

2950 • OUR THOUGHTS?

It may be that the brain is simply a receiving mechanism for thought patterns that originate every where but inside our heads

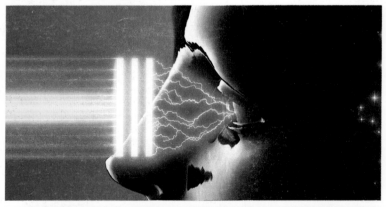

2960 • KNOWING

Psychic abilities will one day open up a whole pot of honey, but maybe also a hornet's nest

2975 • TREE-TALK

Imagine talking to your friend in another town using a tree as your communication system!

THE NOW AGE

AT THE START OF THE 21st century we sampled Rupert Sheldrake's *Principles of Universal Habit*. Throughout the book we have come forward with his theories and looked at them in the light of progress and development in a world where we believe they will be one of the prime interests of science and philosophy.

During the writing of the book the authors have had a number of discussions with Sheldrake, extrapolating from his basic hypothesis into various areas of life and it seems worth including in this last century at the close of the next millennium, those discussions.

Our final abstractions are set out here as they occurred between the authors and Sheldrake.

QUESTION: Can we say that the form-fields present throughout the universe are responsible for and adapted by *all* habits? And that this interconnection can formulate fresh forms in matters such as emotions, diseases, city or home atmospheres etc. In this event would it be correct to say that for the disease AIDS to have come about, there might have formed morphogenetic habits such as stress, sexual repression, homosexual anxiety, drug abuse etc. etc., and that these forms are exacerbated by the fear engendered in the knowledge that the disease exists; i.e. we make AIDS and then feed its forms by fearing it?

Can we also apply this to say New York City or London or a rural landscape in so far as people who have the fitting form-fields for stressful activity or money-making or excitement will be attracted to New York and therefore contribute to its "atmosphere" and conversely those who enjoy peace, quiet etc., would contribute to that state in the countryside?

SHELDRAKE: I think all habits are associated with

207

morphic fields. The interconnection of habits can indeed create the circumstances in which new fields can arise — much of the evolutionary process is of this nature — as habits (such as sexual promiscuity, IV drug use etc.) provide the circumstances in which AIDS could arise. But the habits would not *create* it — new patterns arise through creative steps which are not just a repetition of what went before. The AIDS syndrome, like other diseases, may involve a morphic field as well as germs.

I think the fields of places, such as New York City, or of a temple, or shrine, or cathedral, or haunted house, may indeed have some kind of "memory" which is part of their atmosphere. This, however, goes beyond the more rigorous morphic field concept — partly because of the difficulty in defining when the field of a place begins and ends — in buildings and cities its clear enough, and maybe in valleys, but in relatively featureless countryside it is more difficult.

QUESTION: It is said that emotionally, a divorced individual following a marriage of more than five years, will take at least three years to recover. Could we say that this has a form-field aspect — that the combined forms of the couple take some time to reform?

SHELDRAKE: Assuming that relationships place individuals with higher-level fields — e.g. a wife is part of a family-field, then breaking out of such fields — by divorce or by widowhood, etc., — leaves a great many aspects of habitual response unanswered. It takes time to adjust to changes in habits and conditions of life, in other words, which is common sense, because in common sense we take habits for granted.

QUESTION: If we apply your theory to particle observation — i.e. the scientist/observer, when "looking" at a sub-atomic particle, in becoming part of that experiment, creates a form-field which *is* the looking — thus influencing the particle etc., can we say that this form-field may indeed be creating the particle and the scientist? (This is somewhat

related to the meta-physical concept of "becoming" each moment etc.) — and if so, can we therefore suppose that *all* science is being created in just this way at every moment?

And — can we therefore say that scientific research is in some way a self-replicating phenomenon which has nothing to do with progress but with a God-like and continuous creativity, totally motivated and processed by the "observer" and the forms that "habit" him or her?

SHELDRAKE: I think habits of expectation and observation can influence not just our experience but what happens in the world. But it would be going too far in the direction of solipsism to say that rather trivial habits — of observation in labs — create particles and scientists. Both are sustained by far older and stronger habits — the scientist or a person, for example, has many strong habits which persist independent of observing particular particles.

If science is involved in some way creating the world by theories creating phenomena, then all experiments to test theories would work — but they don't. Experimental tests have an unpredictable quality which suggests the habits of nature have an autonomy that goes beyond mere human expectations. Gravitational forces existed before Newton, and genes before Mendel.

QUESTION: Given that this may be so — how do you fit into the picture? If you created morphogenetic fields by hypothesizing their existence, and as a result they come into existence — surely the creation of them was a form-field in itself so that your new form-field of morphogenesis gave birth to the universe at that moment as a morphogenetic phenomenon. I.e. the universe changed completely with your suggestion.

SHELDRAKE: If morphic resonance occurs, it has always been happening; I have not invented the habit principle, but merely contributed towards an awareness of it in nature and human life.

FINAL ABSTRACTION

SHELDRAKE: The power of prayer is surely the most usual way — practiced by millions if not billions of people — in which people try to affect the course of events through a co-creative process with God, Mary, angels, spirits etc. So ESP, clairvoyance, as well as miracles, are just aspects of a far wider process by which things are believed to be — and I think are — changed by out intentions etc. But not all prayers work! There is an autonomy, again, over and above what we desire, pray and hope for.

QUESTION: Would you say that a genuine appreciation of such phenomenon as form-fields, in terms of your view of them, might lead some time in the future to a desire to control them — i.e. create fresh form for specific purposes? Or, does a genuine appreciation of them dismiss this possibility as "un-morphogenetic?" I.e. by injecting greed or other "negative" human tendencies into the forms around us, we necessarily produce a suitable result. Might we see this as instant karma?

SHELDRAKE: We create fresh morphic fields all the time through out personal and social habits, through inventing new ideas, games, works of art, political and economic systems, etc. All then, like exciting morphic systems such as animals, plants, ecosystems etc., can be subject to greed and control — by coming within the scope of greedy intentions. Morphic fields, by their very nature, can be subject to higher-level fields of organization — including those of human economic systems. But there is, of course, no reason to suppose that human systems of political and economic power represent the highest organized levels in the universe!

QUESTION: Does all this lead us to compare science with the mystic Eastern attitude — that we are "Goding" the universe at every moment and in some way helping to create it, being created within it?

SHELDRAKE: We are only creating or co-creating the universe to a limited extent. It has an autonomy which preceded our existence and which can, I believe, get on without us. We did not "God" the flora and fauna of the Amazon into existence — in fact we are doing the reverse, Goding them out of existence!

QUESTION: Seen from the micro-cosmic point of view all this is more easily imagined but surely it can also apply at the macro-cosmic end of the scale — it is only that we do not have the instruments to measure our affect on say, a tree or star. Nevertheless, when we look at or touch or simply remain in the presence of all events, they change. This might also encompass astrology, tarot, ESP, clairvoyance etc.

R E M E M B E R I N G
THE GOD THOUGHTS

WE HAVE LOOKED NOW, throughout this book at many new theories. The main themes have been attached to a very large extent to the ideas of two bright lights in the scientific world — Rupert Sheldrake and David Bohm — whose theories the author has chosen as the most prominent in the closing years of the 20th century. We have extended their hypotheses through various areas of life involving the brain, the habits of mankind and his relationship with the universe. As we have seen, should these theories become established scientific reality, many things will change and our view of the cosmos may be a totally different one before the next millennium ends.

But one of the most significant aspects of the beliefs that they are beginning to generate is that concerned with man's evolution. As briefly touched upon in the first two pages of this chapter, Sheldrake suggests, in answer to one of the author's questions, that form-fields exist in many different types. There are higher forms, presumably those that have been around for a long time, and then there are varying degrees of lower forms which may be being created all the time.

An example of a fairly high form might, for example, be that of the creation of water from hydrogen and oxygen. Presumably this form has been around since at least the beginning of Earth itself and perhaps before that on other worlds. Still higher forms would be the morphogenesis of stars and planets themselves and still higher those of the creation of hydrogen atoms and other very basic atomic structures within the ancient universe. These forms have had plenty of practice and their formation takes place on a moment by moment basis without effort as their habitual existence is the very foundation of all life.

All this constant formation, then, also carries with it the whole aspect of formulated memory. If habits are always the same habits — i.e. hydrogen and oxygen always somewhere results in the same water — then this memory has also been around as long as the water itself. The memory associated with the creation of stars and planets is an even longer one and the memory for the atomic creation of hydrogen itself may be one of the oldest of all memories.

If we look at memory in this way it becomes then, a morphogenetic field itself — the form-field of memory. We could, for the sake of giving it due respect, call it God's memory.

We are now entering a time in the future when the past has become something so ancient that it precedes all existence — when the concept of memory is more crusty and antiquated, more dark and deep than any ghost or religion or any Egyptian tomb, for such memory is in the very dungeons of life itself. At some time in the very most distant past there would have to have been a form-field created for the purpose of keeping memory — the memory-field. This field would be applied

to all things in order that habit could occur at all. Without it habit would not happen and everything would simply occur in a random aspect without connection or respect for continuity. Such a thing is theoretically as possible as the formation of memory. There could also be a non-memory form or a forget-form. Nature and the universe decided to remember God's memory.

Here, of course, we are totally into what Sheldrake terms solipsism, areas of theory which have virtually no grounding in fact or certainty, but then we are dealing with a time in the future where solipsist concepts may be closer to fact than we could imagine possible today.

The idea of God's memory relates also to the whole area of the brain being no more than a receiving mechanism for outside information. If the cosmic environment is made up of countless form-fields of habit — countless memories — and the brain is simply working like an electrical conductor or radio signal receiver — then all God's memories are available to us if we know where to look for them. Our day-to-day activities are governed by thousands of tiny memories. We remember to wash, brush our teeth, eat, sleep. We remember countless facts about life as our brains are called upon at every moment to do so. We summon up a host of information all the time.

All this information within our present state of life is used for the purpose of living the lives we have chosen. If we are working in an office or on a farm or driving a bus etc., all the memories drawn from the brain are needed to do these functions. Most of us spend so much of our energies on mundane and "normal" activities that we have little time to get into anything new or distant from the norm. But for those of us who have meditated there is more. During meditation, especially after some time has been spent in the practice of meditation, new ideas, memories and experiences occur. They very often have nothing whatever to do with the everyday activities of life and can surprise us with their bizarre content. They can even be predictive or irrational in content so that the indications are that there is much more around than we normally experience during daily life.

We might even say that we are probably only in receipt of a minute proportion of all that is available. If we have an unlimited access to the cosmic or God-memory and have chosen at this stage only to tap a small percentage of it, then perhaps by the end of the next millennium we will have woken up to some very dramatic possibilities.

They say in astronomical research, that there is dust in space which still floats about, readily available, that came from the original "big bang" — that this dust came out of the explosion which occurred. In other words we can actually get out there and gather up particles of the first step in our own universal beginning (that is, if this is really the way the universe began).

Perhaps this is also so of memory. If we can develop the memory reception within our brain-receivers to pick up the very earliest habits of the universe, then we will at once be in touch with the earliest of times. We will have, in effect, traveled to the beginning of the universe through our minds.

PSYCHICS IN EVERYTHING

INTRINSIC TO SUCH IDEAS lies the whole field of the para-normal — clairvoyance, ESP, psychic phenomena. We are, in the future, certainly going to see a transformation of subjects such

memories in their identifiable form-fields of past life, then they may be very revealing to those of the future able to track them and identify their character. In simple aspects of criminal research where a murder has taken place, the source of the crime would best be discovered by being able to make contact with the victim. Were we able to get in touch with the dead through provable scientific means we could then literally "question" the victim and get the answers needed to convict the culprit.

Parapsychologists at City College in New York, for example, using the most advanced equipment available in the 20th century, are already deep into the business of ghost-hunting. Using geiger counters and infrared film, ghost-buster Michaeleen Meher, can often be found in buildings where ghosts have been detected. Meher was the inspiration for the movie *Ghostbusters* and provided much of the research material for the scripting of the film.

According to interviews and questionnaires around the United States as many as one third of those interviewed professed to have had some experience of ghostly presences.

The most significant results seem to coincide with emotional situations of greater strength — such as the death of a spouse or some major crime or incidence of anxiety within a haunted building. People who sense the presence of ghosts are very definite about it and can even pinpoint actual locations where the ghostly presences are felt.

The problem today in trying to substantiate these claims seems to be the lack of precise and usable instrumentation. How, after all, do you track a ghost with something when you don't know what you need to track it with? In the future, with more sophisticated "morphometers" we may be able to tap directly into form-fields in the environment and therefore find our ghostly presences or clairvoyant subjects or poltergeists, more easily.

as these, from what is today of low-level scientific interest, to one that will probably dominate man's interest in the future. For if we learn that we have a direct correspondence with our environment and with all other living creatures, then we can find out all we need to know without cutting up the world, but simply by communicating with it.

The psychic phenomenon has, during the 20th century, already seen a great leap forward. Even the police forces of the world are quite commonly using clairvoyants to track down criminals, and given a much greater understanding of the phenomenon we may be putting psychics to work in all areas of life.

One of the most revealing possibilities is that of Ghost-hunting or Ghost-busting. If ghosts can be seen as the remaining essences of past

ANGELS
OF
DEATH

necessary then to institute similar processes to those suggested in some science fiction movies where people *must* undergo a physical death at some point during their lives in order to satisfy various phenomena.

There may also be far more remote reasons why we need to face death such as those involved in the cleansing of the spirit suggested by prophets such as Jesus and many of the Eastern religious leaders. Perhaps the angel of death is a necessary addition to life and this will become integrated into the future in the same way as is birth.

After all, if we knew we were definitely coming back for another life after this one, we might have a lot more fun in both lives as the fear of death would then be transformed into something positive and happy. The process of death would happen and we might even find ways of deciding exactly the kind of life we were going to lead next time around.

With the ability to tap into a cosmic memory which presumably would also contain memories of our past lives, there would also be no need to lose touch with the experiences of the previous lives.

The tendency might even arise to want to put an end to one life sooner in order to get on with the next one!

ONE OF THE PROBLEMS THAT will be faced in our last century of the next millennium is that of how to deal with death.

It seems most probable that the whole present effect of death will have changed within the next thousand years. If we can effectively create conditions under which life can continue virtually indefinitely, by the use of cryogenics, test-tube production of the body, new body parts etc., then there will be a whole new question arising as to the purpose of death. Why do we need to die at all? Is there some deeply rooted natural cycle involved in giving up life and if so do we come back through many other lives as the philosophies of reincarnation suggest?

The extension of life into a permanent state might therefore seriously interfere with yet another of nature's normal processes. It may be

A FAMILY OF TREES

BY THE 30TH CENTURY there may be trees on this planet that are over five thousand years on Earth. The "bristle cone" pines in Yosemite, California have already been around for almost 4,600 years today and if we are able to maintain their existence they will certainly be amongst the oldest living "creatures" on Earth in the next millennium.

Given a deeper understanding of those aspects of our environment and their life-ness, we may begin to find new relationships building in the future. There are already those around the world, largely people who are in some way associated with the Eastern philosophies, who state that they have on-going relationships, love affairs and close understandings with trees, plants etc.

Within the American Indian tribes there are methods of communication which occur between members of the tribes using trees as the transmitting power. If one member of the tribe is elsewhere and wishes to send a message back home he will simply go to a particular tree and "tell the tree" the message. Anyone going to a similar breed of tree in the home area will receive the message. The trees that are used for such correspondence are specially grown and each new tree is sprouted from the branches of the other such trees. The ritual surrounding the care of such trees is a religious one and the whole contact between the people and their "talking" trees is preserved with great reverence.

To the Western mind such an idea is bizarre in the least but if we look at it in a different light it becomes less peculiar.

Consider the radio or television or telephone. If you did not know what these instruments were and how they worked, you might have some doubts as to their powers. You might watch someone talking into a telephone — speaking to a piece of plastic — and wonder how on earth such a thing could happen. Without knowing the method by which a radio receives radio waves you might well doubt its authenticity and call it equally as bizarre as a talking tree.

There may be invisible forces, as we have discussed in other areas, and it may also be simply that we have not come across the means by which a tree can communicate with other trees and with people and animals.

There is plenty of other evidence of the communications between animals and plants and between plants and humans — such as those stories told by Lyall Watson in his various and fascinating books. There are the tales of plants knowing the humans who have killed other plants and of the Kudu animals in Africa eating from trees that literally warn other trees in the area to poison their leaves against being over-eaten.

Perhaps in the far distant future we will begin to become part of the family of trees and the family of all other living creatures and plants — or even the rocks and the earth itself.

A S A FINAL POINT OF INTEREST for *The History of the Future* we will end this book with the basic and most life-giving substance in the universe — light.

Light was one of the very first items to be provided on this planet and within the knowable universe. Without light we could not live for it provides heat, sight and inspiration to the entire planet. We use it as a barrier for much of physics for the magic number of 186,000 miles per second has formed a certainty for the whole of the physical sciences.

Although we now suspect that there may be particles that travel at 187,000 miles per second or more, we know still with some certainty that nothing can actually travel *at* the speed of light for at this speed the substances simply become too massive to survive. But light manages!

One of the prime sources of light that will interest mankind in the far future is that of the stars and one of the most revealing aspects of a star's life-span comes from our modern observation of supernovae — though it must be said that there have not been many exploding stars to observe in recent years. The death of a star is a major event and perhaps it is worth just passing mention of how one of the prime sources of light in our universe passes through its time.

The Supernova Shelton, the most recent of observed exploding stars (watched during its explosive cycle by the star watcher Ian Shelton — a self-educated astronomer from New York, working in Chile) probably began its life some 13 million years before its death, as clouds of primordial hydrogen rising in temperature through the contractions of gravity to around 30 million degrees. At this temperature a chemical fusion takes place and the hydrogen becomes helium. During the reaction, light and heat are emitted and the star begins to shine. The energy released stops any further collapse of the star for as long as the fusion continues and in this way all stars of this magnitude continue to shine in our skies. They are all in effect giant fusion bombs burning up over millions of years.

Subsequently, about one million years before its death, Supernova Shelton began to contract further because of the heavier helium element and the temperature increased to 150 million degrees. With such heat carbon forms, liberating new energy, hydrogen continues to fuse at the edges of the star making more helium. Six thousand years before the end the contraction reached a point where the temperature had risen to over 600 million

LET THERE BE LIGHT

degrees, and the carbon fused to become neon and the earlier fusions of hydrogen to helium and helium to carbon continued on the edge.

Seven years before the supernova the temperature had reached 1.3 billion degrees and the neon became oxygen and one year before death the oxygen would fuse to silicon at 1.9 billion degrees. Time ever shortening now, three days before the end the core would shrink under heat of 3 billion degrees and silicon becomes iron. Now iron cannot spontaneously fuse into another form and so the central core of the star remains iron and this marks the impending end of the star.

Two hundred milliseconds before the end the iron has become so massive within the star that there is not enough energy to support the star at all so that it begins to collapse from within — temperatures rising to over 8 billion degrees! Within the next moments the star shrinks at a speed which is only one quarter of the speed of light and becomes as small as six miles in diameter to what scientists call the "maximum scrunch". From here the star begins exploding outwards again through the massive internal pressure which gives off more energy than comes from an entire galaxy in one full year. The shock waves rush outwards at speeds of over eleven thousand miles per second and within an hour of the initial explosion the energy form is moving a little slower than initially and becomes light. It is at this point that the supernova becomes visible to the naked eye.

The resulting mass that is blown into space by the dead star is exactly that which is the stuff of life. Stars give us everything we need to exist, including light.

But what is most dramatic and extraordinary is the fact that Supernova Shelton, viewed in 1987 by Ian Shelton happened 170,000 years ago! In other words it is more than 31 million million miles away and the event of its death occurred so long ago that in that region of space there is certainly no trace of its ever having been there. And yet we, here on Earth are only aware of its passing now. All the evidence, the light and the materials that this star exploded into are in our existential presence today.

So the light that we receive from supernovae is history — long past history and yet it continues to give us power and life thousands of years beyond its death.

In the distant future, one thousand years from now we may have found a way of traveling faster than light but we will never be able to view an exploding star until long long after it has gone for without light we cannot see what has gone before.

AND AS A LAST THOUGHT before the last pages we might consider this — that everything we see, therefore, is only ever seen after it has gone. The time between the events that are close to us and our vision of them may only be infinitesimally small but it exists nevertheless. The speed of light entering into our seeing senses plus the time needed to translate the image into something recognizable, (compare it with our references of awareness) all takes a split millisecond, by which time the event has already passed. We look at a flower by the road or a person in front of us and by the time we have digested the event it has gone. Flowers change, people change. We see only the past, never the present and certainly never the future.

Our predictions are an attempt to travel faster than light — and the further ahead we go into the future the faster we are attempting to travel until we reach speeds that are far in excess of anything in the known universe. We are acting like a supernova in reverse in our attempts to see what may come. At least if we consider time and speed in a linear mode. It is said that prophets such as Nostradamus and Edgar Cayce did not view time in any passing and linear fashion but more simply had access to a different dimension — one that brought the far future into their grasp because of other phenomena that they and we still know nothing of.

Perhaps the theories of Sheldrake, Bohm and others point towards a future that is already written in some way within the holographic fabric of the universe.

But in any event, the intention of this book has not been to create any sound picture of the actual future, but to draw a picture which represents one of the alternatives we may face. There has been so much talk and expectation of disaster in the last few decades, brought about to a great extent by fear and apprehension of annihilation, that the author

felt there might be some place for a more positive scheme of life to come. No doubt it will be labeled utopic by some for whenever we attempt to be positive about the future that is almost invariably the criticism. The human race is much more at home with negative values than with hope and joy. A bad future gives the human race something to get their teeth into. The worse it is going to be the better for then there is room for the ego to make its mark. If life is going to be so good what is the human "I" going to do?!

Nostradamus was extremely clear about the way life can unfold. He stated that the future could go two ways only — the alternatives becoming clear at around the turn of the 20th century, a time of major transition. One way to go would be total annihilation by nuclear destruction. And his quatrains draw a realistic picture of this choice, leaving little or nothing behind to pick up the pieces. The other alternative was a raising of consciousness. An increased awareness that mankind *is* nature, *is* God, and the resulting change in life, would bring about a diversion from the inevitable destructive end to Earth.

There are others today who say that it is already too late. That the damage we have done is already beyond reversion. Masters such as U.G.Krishnamurti offer no hope at all, stating that we may just manage to elevate ourselves sufficiently to leave the planet with some grace while all else is falling about our ears, but that is the best we can expect. Perhaps this is so. And perhaps it is important that we recognize such a possibility for most of us have the tendency to think — ah well, everything will turn out OK —

FINAL MOMENTS

nature is too strong to be beaten by mere humans and their foolish ways. And it is this idea that is bringing us closer and closer to the time when "nature" says enough — time for human life to go! We all have a part to play in the return to sanity.

So, the 30th century may be a utopia by comparison with the dark ages of the 20th century. It may be an empty planet, or one occupied by a totally different race of people from elsewhere in the universe, mankind gone forever. Or it may be a mixture of the two — happy and unhappy, inter-mixed and solitary, living and dying, just as it is today.

EPILOG

Australopithecus

2.6 million years B.C.

The first signs of mankind known today were discovered by Raymond Dart in 1924 at Taungs, Transvaal — tool-making hominids.

Pleistocene Age

600,000 years B.C. — 10,000 years B.C.

Mankind developed from primitive hominids to the Upper Old Stone Age — Homo sapiens sapiens.

Mesolithic Middle Stone Age

10,000 years B.C. — 2nd millennium B.C.

Mesolithic and Neolithic Man developed as the ice-ages receded to the north. The life for man was based on hunting, fishing and gathering conditions but as the climate became warmer, nomadic tribes settled in more fixed areas of the planet.

The Bronze Age

3,500—800 B.C.

In this age came the development of metal as tools and ornaments. Metals used were copper, bronze, gold, silver and lead. Centers of mankind's activity were in Germany, Bohemia and Austria.

The Iron Age

From 800 B.C.
Life expanded within old Europe.

The Early Empires

3,000—330 B.C.

Egypt, Mesopotamia, Indo-Europe, Asia Minor, Palestine, Phoenicia, China, India, Persia. Life developed across the globe.

Antiquity — Greece

Mycenaean Epoch — 2,500—323 B.C.

Known as the migrations period with tribes coming from various parts of the world to Greece and surrounding areas.

The Hellenistic Age

323—280 B.C.
Macedonia and Alexander the Great.

The Age of Rome

1,000—500 B.C.
Etruscans — Early period. Rome becomes established in the Etruscan Age.

The State of Rome

500—30 B.C.

From the beginning of the State of Rome to the second civil wars that began its downfall.

The Early Middle Ages

Christianity — 1—375 A.D.
Rome gives way to Europe and the Middle Ages begin with Christianity growing some two hundred years after the death of Christ.

THE AGES OF MANKIND

The Barbarian Migrations

375—568 A.D.

The tribes of the barbarians such as the Bastarnae, the Skiri and the Cimbri move across the Middle East and Europe, defeating the Romans and causing devastation wherever they go.

Early Germanic States

—Occupants of Europe — 400—1066 A.D.

European nations begin to be established — France, Germany and England. The form of life was feudalism during this period — i.e. local areas controlled by Lords and the land worked by farming peasants.

Early Middle Ages Completing

1066—1300 A.D.

Period of the Middle Ages moves through to the High Middle Ages and the beginning of the Late Middle Ages. This period including the German Empire, the Late Ottoman Empire and the transitions in England to the beginning of the Renaissance.

The Age of Humanism

Renaissance — 1526—1658 A.D.

This extraordinary age was also known as the Age of Transition for its movement away from slaughter and blood to that of the intellect and art. It changed the whole of Europe and much of the East and Far East with a mass of genius and creative growth throughout the world.

The Age of Religious Discord

—1648 A.D.

Moving alongside the Age of Transition came the religious changes brought about by Martin Luther, The Spanish Inquisition and the Catholic Renewal. In this time was the Thirty Years War and it is interesting to note how the Age of Transition brought much war then, as it is during the 20th century.

The Age of Reason

1648 — 1800 A.D.

Also known as the Age of Enlightenment the term refers to the development of mankind within the national communities, including the birth of the United States of America so late in our history.

The Age of Revolution

1792 — 1945 A.D.

From this age onwards we see almost permanent war and depression, with the American Revolution, the Napoleonic Wars, The British Empire, Imperialism, The Boa Wars, The First and Second World Wars, The Vietnam War and today the almost constant War of the Terrorists. This period began with The Age of Revolution and has continued through the following ages —

The Napoleonic Age

Age of Restoration and Revolution

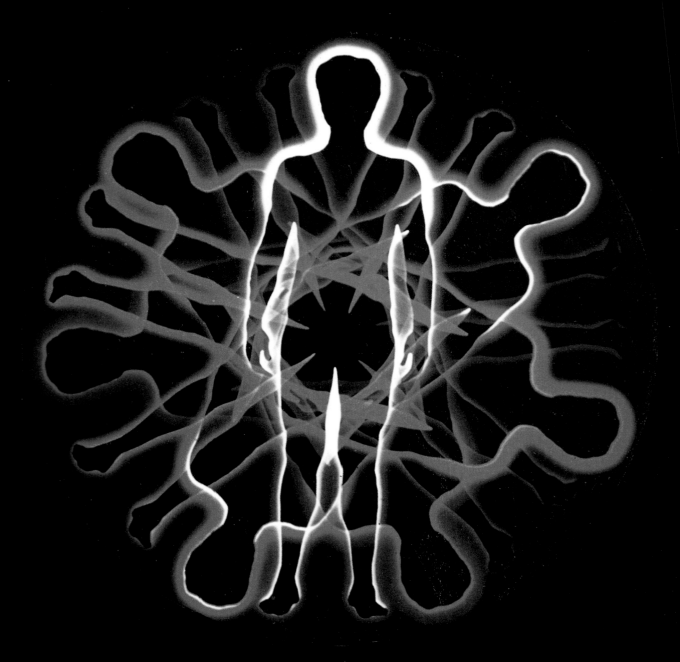

Age of the National States

The Age of Imperialism

The First and Second World War Ages

This period of time included more depression and chaos than almost any age of mankind in the past.

The Age of Transition

1945—2006 A.D.

Here there is a growth point to critical mass, as the evolutionists would have it — with a crossroad to either complete chaos or change for the better; with political dissatisfaction, ecological disaster, Human Potential Movements, The New Age and all the possibilities of which way to go leading out of the second millennium after Christ.

The Age of Acceptance

2006—2,200

The death of organized religion and the acceptance of enlightenment as the way to go forward. Mankind begins to make some sense out of his existence.

The Age of The Heart

2,200—2,300

Silence and the end of reason as a power. The beginnings of World Government and a possible world peace lead mankind into areas of life hitherto never suspected to be possible.

The Age of Global Madness

2,300—2,400

Life takes a sudden dip from the previous age of hope and glory and turns to a number of new choices — galactic contact with other species, time travel and hints of new sciences.

The Half Millennium

2,400—2,500

New planets to live upon, the fulfillment of science as a partner to religion — the philo-sciences and the power of womanhood.

The Age of Confidence

2,500—2,600

War again after hundreds of years of relative peace, comes through contact with other planets and species and mankind's excessive confidence in himself and his growth. Leisure and time off become a problem as machines and robots take over the work.

The Age of Magic

2,600—2,700

Witchcraft and the old dark sciences rear their heads and become established methods of understanding life. The wholeness of the universe is an accepted way of life and mankind fulfills another of his ambitions — the arrival of a complete universe.

Breaking Away

2,700—2,800

Moving away from Earth, leaving behind a silent minority of meditators while the more active population searches for new worlds to live upon.

A Quiet Earth

2,800—2,900

Perhaps for the first time in thousands of years there is finally peace on Earth as most of the human race departs.

The Closing Millennium

2,900—3,000

The last years before 3,000 see Earth enjoying the new sciences and the central issues of life.

ACKNOWLEDGEMENTS

The author would like to thank all those at Labyrinth Publishing and The Master's Press for their work in compiling this book and their joy for life. Also Rupert Sheldrake for his specially written piece on The Principles of Universal Habit and his answers to the various questions of the author on the subject of Morphological form-fields. Also to Dr. Landert for his help with global financial futures.

The publishers wish to acknowledge the following agencies and copyright holders for their granted permissions of the use of certain illustrations in the book:

Yatri, Tuscany, Italy: *Front Cover, Back Cover, 57, 58, 110, 111, 121, 157,163, 164.*
Gianluca De Santis, Calci, Italy: *12/13, 166, 170, 184, 210, 205.*
Padma Morgan, Labyrinth Publishing, Switzerland: *34, 55, 150, 178/179.*
A.J. Sullivan, Newton Highlands, Massachusetts: *39.*
Anthony Gormley, London: *172/173*
Bruno Kortenhorst, Labyrinth Publishing, Switzerland: *203.*
Rajneesh Foundation, Poona, India: *29.*
Susan Griggs Agency, London: *78.*
GSF Picture Library, England: *120.*
Arcaid, Kingston, London, England: *78.*
Nino Millemaci, Pisa, Italy: *212/213.*
Le Campion/ANA, Paris: *135.*
Denjiro/GIP/Speranza, Italy: *104.*
Len Sirman Press, Switzerland: *195.*
Massini/Phototake, New York: *126.*
Francesco Garufi/Lucky Star/Dossier, Italy: *40.*
Micheal Whelan, Connecticut: *102, 139.*
VLOO/Marka, Italy: *10.*
TPS/ICP, Italy: *140.*
Craig Aurness/West Lights/G.Neri, Italy: *71.*
Robin Hiddon/Young Artists, London: *76/77.*
Chris Newbert, Hawaii: *70.*
Jean Delville, "I Tesori di Satana", 1895: *146*